C000132225

Publish and Flourish

A CONSULTANT'S GUIDE

How to Boost Visibility and Earnings through a Publishing Strategy

Garry Schaeffer
Dr. Tony Alessandra

John Wiley & Sons, Inc.
New York • Chichester • Brisbane • Toronto • Singapore

In recognition of the importance of preserving what has been written, it is a policy of John Wiley & Sons, Inc., to have books of enduring value printed on acid-free paper, and we exert our best efforts to that end.

Copyright © 1992, Garry Schaeffer and Dr. Tony Alessandra
Published by John Wiley & Sons, Inc.

All rights reserved. Published simultaneously in Canada.

Reproduction or translation of any part of this work beyond that permitted by Section 107 or 108 of the 1976 United States Copyright Act without the permission of the copyright owner is unlawful. Requests for permission or further information should be addressed to the Permissions Department, John Wiley & Sons, Inc.

This publication is designed to provide accurate and authoritative information in regard to the subject matter covered. It is sold with the understanding that the publisher is not engaged in rendering legal, accounting, or other professional service. If legal advice or other expert assistance is required, the services of a competent professional person should be sought. *From a Declaration of Principles jointly adopted by a Committee of the American Bar Association and a Committee of Publishers.*

Library of Congress Cataloging-in-Publication Data:

Schaeffer, Garry.
   Publish and flourish—a consultant's guide : how to boost
visibility and earnings through a publishing strategy / Garry
Schaeffer, Tony Alessandra.
     p.   cm.
   Includes index.
   ISBN 0-471-57116-4 (cloth)
   1. Business writing—Handbooks, manuals, etc. 2. Business—
Research—Handbooks, manuals, etc. 3. Business literature—
Publishing—Handbooks, manuals, etc. 4. Consultants—
Handbooks, manuals, etc. I. Alessandra, Anthony J. II. Title.
HF5718.3.S3   1992
001'.068'8—dc20   91-39636
                                           CIP

Printed in the United States of America

10 9 8 7 6 5 4 3 2 1

CONTENTS

PART TWO: START WITH ARTICLES

PART THREE: MOVE ON TO YOUR BOOK

PART FOUR: DEVELOP THE SKILLS
OF A SUCCESSFUL WRITER

PART FIVE: MAKE A NAME FOR YOURSELF

Garry Schaeffer thanks Barbara, Allan, Shirley, and Erwin for their loving support

PREFACE

This book was written to solve a problem: the dead end that confronts many consultants, professional speakers, and trainers after several years in the business. Many people get to a point in which they are established, but not to the extent that they would like. The question becomes, *How do I make the leap to the position of having nearly all the business I want?* The answer is simple: Get published.

This book will teach you how to write articles and books. It will take you through all the steps—from getting motivated and understanding why you *must* write and get published, to the conceptualization and research of your article or book, to the actual writing and marketing of the finished product.

Simply reading this book will not do a thing for you. You must work it. Follow our advice and work hard through each step. Only then will you break through the literary and career barriers that have held you back until now.

To make your task easier, at the end of each chapter, you will find a section called Small Steps To Success. It will list activities to do and ask you to set target dates for their completion. Set dates and complete all of the small increments that we suggest. You will be rewarded by quickly and easily mastering the skills necessary to write quality articles and books.

We make only one apology at this point. All writers have to grapple with the issue of gender. We regret that an easy answer does not exist. English is one of the least sex-conscious languages. Unlike French, German, and Spanish, which attribute masculinity and femininity to all nouns, English is sexist with only a few pronouns, so writers are continually confronted with the choice of writing *he* or *she*. Alternating between the two becomes awkward, so for consistency we have chosen to use the traditional *he*, but not without some obvious self-consciousness. The decision was based solely on the desire to make this book as reader friendly as possible. If you are offended, please take consolation in our intention to use *she* exclusively in our next book.

INTRODUCTION

You were not born knowing how to give business advice, deliver a keynote speech, or conduct a training seminar. Writers are not born knowing how to express themselves clearly or with pizzazz.

You have probably achieved the formidable goal of being able to give a presentation, so there is no reason that you cannot learn to write—unless you let your fears get in the way.

Being a consultant, professional speaker, or trainer gives you a marked advantage. You have already overcome the fear of presenting your thoughts for public consumption or speaking in front of a group. Now you can overcome your fear of writing, but first you have to learn how.

Fear is an emotion of anticipation. You look at the future and imagine a bad scenario. Unfounded fears, especially the general fear of failure, cause you to freeze or give your work only a half-hearted effort.

This common roadblock has several causes. The most obvious is a pessimistic, overactive imagination. Another is a lack of awareness of the steps needed to achieve success. Rather than risk taking the wrong steps, some people do nothing at all—a response that limits growth and perpetuates stagnation. It is better to act and fail than to be passive. Failure provides feedback that can help you succeed in the future; inertia offers no insight and advances nothing.

These generalizations apply to writing articles and books as they do to any other endeavor in life. The most difficult step for new writers is to overcome inertia; it requires the most energy. Again, this is partly due to ignorance. Launching a book project, in particular, carries with it many unknowns. How much work will it take? Will I have enough time and self-discipline to complete the project? Will I be able to do a credible job? Will it pay off in the long run?

A powerful method for eliminating fears in your life is to complete the sentence: "I am scaring myself by imagining that . . ." Fill in the blank as many times as you can with those self-defeating internal sentences that short-circuit your determination. Write them down and analyze them. Then treat them as you would any other useless garbage that clutters your life: Discard them.

Here are some examples of fearful thoughts and how this book will allay them:

"I scare myself by imagining that I don't have the self-discipline to write a book." See Chapter 2, "Writing Is a Mental Game."

"I scare myself by imagining that I can't write well." Chapters 4, 7, 8, and 14, which cover research, writing techniques, editing, and writing with style, will help lay this fear to rest.

"I scare myself by imagining that I don't have the time to write a book." Nonsense. Chapters 15 and 16 will teach you how to speed the process. You can also use time management techniques, books on which are readily available.

"I scare myself by imagining that a book will turn out badly." Help is on the way. See Chapter 9 on collaborations.

"I scare myself by imagining that no publisher will be interested in my book." Chapter 12 will show you the advantages of self-publishing. Chapter 18 will give you insight into marketing your book and yourself.

Finish this book before you worry any more about the frightening details. Your fears will disappear after you have read and applied its lessons.

USE YOUR VERBAL SKILLS TO DEVELOP
WRITING SKILLS

As a consultant, speaker, or trainer, you are in the enviable position of already being bright and articulate. Writing and speaking are remarkably similar. The only difference is in delivery. The two processes are quite similar—and many people believe writing is easier. If you can speak to colleagues or an audience, you can learn to speak to readers on paper.

   If you are like many people who freeze when confronted with the task of writing, rest assured that this book will drive a stake through the heart of your fear. We will show you how to be more productive and creative—and how to sell what you write.

PART ONE

Of Course You Can Do It

1

WHY YOU *MUST* GET PUBLISHED

The ideal reason to publish articles and books is to contribute something original to the body of knowledge in your field. That's the ideal. Now, let's get real. Thousands of articles and books are published each year, and few of them say anything truly original. Therefore, the primary criterion for publishability—from the publisher's standpoint—must not be originality; it is—like marketing any product or service—salability. Lucky for you! Having a salable idea is far easier than having an original idea.

From your point of view, there are several salient reasons to get published. It increases your credibility, creates visibility, allows you to raise your fees, serves as a powerful promotional tool, and generates passive income. Most of these benefits apply to books, but they also apply to articles, although to a lesser degree.*

---

*We don't want you to think you must tackle a book first. Writing articles is a good way to get your feet wet and build your writing confidence.

RAISE YOUR FEES

We thought you'd want to know about this first. As a consultant, speaker, or trainer who has published, you will be perceived by your colleagues and clients as an expert. Your book will give you credibility and help thrust you into the upper echelons of your profession.

Consultants and others who have written books, especially books that have sold well, can command dramatically higher fees than before their books were published. Ken Blanchard is a well-known case in point. After *The One-Minute Manager* (Morrow, 1981) hit the bookstores, his speaking fees immediately doubled. Tony Alessandra is another good example of the impact of books on speaking fees. Between 1979, when his first book came out, and 1984, when his third book was published, his fees increased 500 percent.

BUSINESS WILL COME TO YOU

It's truly exciting to be able to ask for more money and get it. It's also quite flattering to have prospective clients call *you* and mention that they saw or read your book.

When a prospect calls you to inquire about your services, you have the upper hand. The deal is easier to sell and negotiate than if you had called him, especially unsolicited. No one likes to qualify a prospect or bend over backward to convince him that you are an authority in your field. Those days will be over. Your credibility will be immediately established by your book or article.

YOUR MOST POWERFUL PROMOTIONAL TOOL

A book is better than a brochure. It will save you time on the telephone. You know how difficult it can be to explain your program or services succinctly to someone over the telephone. Even if you could adequately convey the essence of your expertise, clients often tune you out or forget what you've said.

People who hire consultants, trainers, and speakers are often shopping around. They want to know what differentiates you from any competitors they may be considering. Imagine how easy it will become when you can say, "Let me send you a copy of my book."

The average brochure probably ends up in the wastebasket

within ten minutes of being taken out of the envelope. How many people do you think would throw away a book? Very few. People generally put books on bookshelves—if for no other reason than to appear well read—so your book-as-brochure will have a longer shelf life than the typical brochure.

PASSIVE INCOME

Book sales will increase your passive income. Granted, you probably won't get rich, but remember that your primary reason for getting published is not money but increased visibility, which could make you rich.

To maximize your profits from book sales, strike a deal with your publisher that allows you to buy books at a substantial discount. Then promote and sell them yourself. The profit margin on books you sell will be far greater than the royalties you earn from books sold in retail stores. In addition, your publisher will appreciate your efforts to promote yourself and, if you sell a lot of books, will look forward to publishing more of your work.

Over the years Tony Alessandra has coauthored many books, one of which, *Non-Manipulative Selling*, has sold more than 100,000 copies. Tony believes his efforts are responsible for the sale of more than 75,000 of those copies. He has received orders for hundreds and even thousands of copies at a time from companies that want to give a book to all their salespeople. One company alone ordered 10,500 books for its employees, representing an instant profit of thousands of dollars for Tony.

CREATIVE MARKETING FOR YOUR SERVICES

Having a book gives you creative angles with which to get work. It gives you the ability to offer special deals to your clients. For example, you might offer to:

• **Sell the books retail.** Reduce or eliminate your usual fee if the company will buy one copy of your book for every person in the audience. Before making such an agreement, you need to know how many people will be in attendance or get a commitment for a guaranteed minimum quantity of books.

Multiply the number of audience members by your profit per

book. Often you will make more money than if you charged a flat fee. Let's say your client expects 300 people. Your profit on each book is $5 (hypothetically), so you will make $1,500 for the session—a respectable fee. If you can negotiate a fee on top of the book sales, you are really doing well.

There is another benefit to this strategy: Clients often perceive your services as a terrific deal because the book has increased your value beyond what is normally given.

• **Sell the books at a discount.** Charge your regular fee, sell the books to your client at a discount, and distribute the books during or after your presentation. Your client will be delighted to receive a discount and will like the idea of everyone having something to keep the ideas alive after you have left.

• **Include books for free.** Entice your prospect by telling him you will give everyone a free book as part of your program. To include a copy of your book for each attendee, multiply your cost per book by the number to be given away, and add that figure to your fee.

Each of these strategies can encourage an uncertain prospect to choose you rather than a competitor. As you raise the perceived value of your programs, you will increase your bookings.

EXPAND YOUR BUSINESS

At the end of a speech or seminar, mention that your book is available for a modest price: "I have a book that goes into more detail on the subject I spoke about today. If you're interested in getting a copy, give me your business card, and I'll have my office send a copy along with an invoice." This strategy works better than asking people to pay in advance. Two hypothetical scenarios will illustrate the psychological dynamics involved.

Let's say you have the books with you to sell on the spot. If you ask for immediate payment, you may sell, say, ten books. Your book sells for $20, and your cost is $8; your profit will be $12 × 10 books, or $120.

The other strategy is to give away books and invoice people later or take business cards and ship the books and invoices later. There is a psychological advantage to taking business cards instead of money. People are more inclined to give you a business card. There is no commitment in doing so. So you will collect more business cards than money. Let's say you collect twenty business cards and later ship twenty books. Your cost for the books would be $160. Realistically, you cannot expect to be paid by every buyer—some people will never pay—but let's say sixteen of the twenty pay their invoices. Your gross receipts would be $320, with a profit of $160. The second method yielded a 30 percent greater profit despite the bad debts. Furthermore, the four books that went unpaid still serve as promotional tools and may stimulate future business.

A variation of the second strategy will eliminate bad debts. Instead of shipping a book with an invoice, send a letter to each person. Tell him that you will rush a book as soon as you receive payment. Give customers the option of calling your office collect for credit card orders. To make your sales letter even more effective, insert a brochure about the book and a copy of a favorable review. Always offer an unconditional money-back guarantee.

There is one more advantage to collecting business cards—your mailing list. Take all those cards and add them to your computerized prospect database. These are people who may be interested in your future products.

HOW YOU ARE ALREADY QUALIFIED TO WRITE A BOOK

Writing a book requires only three things: expertise in some area, the ability to communicate in writing, and the willingness to spend the time required to do the work.

As a businessperson, you are already an expert in your field, and you have the ability to communicate verbally, which is 95 percent of writing well. Anyone who has the talent and communication skills necessary to talk to an audience for an hour has more than enough talent to write a book.

The third requirement for writing a book—putting in the time—will come easily as you increase your motivation to create the time to complete your book. You will find writing a book to be easier than you imagined after you have learned how to increase your productivity.

One thing you will read repeatedly in this book:

> **The key to writing a book successfully
> is to break it down into small,
> manageable increments.**

Believe it.

Work on the Small Steps to Success that appear at the end of each chapter. Be patient. Commit yourself to your new undertaking, and have fun with the writing process.

2

WRITING IS A MENTAL GAME

What is the difference between someone who accomplishes a great deal and someone who does little? Is it intelligence, time management, motivation, or a combination of all three? The answer varies from person to person, but the most powerful factor is motivation. Motivation pushes you to do what you have to do to get to where you want to be.

What is motivation? Is it possible to be motivated and lazy at the same time? No. The bottom line is that you are motivated when you care about yourself enough to work hard. There is no such thing as having the intention to do something but being too lazy to accomplish it. Laziness is an excuse for not caring.

To determine your level of motivation, answer yes or no to the following questions (write your answers alongside each question):

1. Is success the most important thing in your life?
2. Are you willing to take responsibility for your accomplishments?
3. Are you interested in being an author and gaining the respect and credibility that will come with that distinction?

4. Are you willing to change your attitude so you will see writing a book as a challenge rather than an arduous task?

5. Do you fully appreciate and understand the significant impact your book will have on your career?

6. Are you willing to make the commitment to work hard and make sacrifices to achieve the status of being a published author?

7. Are you willing to overcome your writing fears, feelings of incompetence, and other obstacles?

If you answered no to any of these questions, reading the rest of this book will change your mind. If you answered yes to all of them, you have taken the first step in overcoming fear and inertia and gaining motivation and momentum toward writing your book. Congratulations! The rest should flow smoothly.

But if you had trouble answering some of the questions and are still not sure how you feel and what you want, do a simple exercise. On a sheet of paper, draw a line vertically down the middle. On the left side of the page, write the heading, "What do I want?" On the right side, write the heading, "What am I willing to settle for?" Start on the left side and write a brief answer to each question; then do the same for the right side. Keep doing it until you come up blank. For example—

What Do I Want?	What Am I Willing to Settle For?
To be famous	A solid career that keeps me busy
To make $350,000 a year	$75,000 a year
To get a book published	Writing a book someday
A 50-foot yacht	Chartering sailboats occasionally
Three children	Two children and a cocker spaniel
A closer relationship with my brother	Talking on the telephone once a week with my brother

You get the idea. As you move through this exercise, you will identify your ambitions and the compromises you are willing or unwilling to make. Don't limit your self-exploration to professional aspirations or material things. Delve into the emotional aspects as well, and you will be surprised how much you learn.

TAKE THE LONG-TERM VIEW

Certainly there is nothing new or profound about the notion that our minds have ultimate control over our actions. A reminder of this principle, however, will serve to bolster your determination and stimulate positive thoughts about the work that lies ahead of you.

In driver education, high school students are taught to focus their eyes well ahead of the car rather than on the road immediately in front of them. This technique gives them a safer perspective and more reaction time because they see the big picture. Bottleneck up ahead? Change lanes and pass everyone.

Life is the same way. Having a myopic outlook puts you at a disadvantage, whereas planning in advance gives you the ability to steer your own course. Wouldn't you rather change lanes and pass the slowpokes rather than be stuck in traffic behind them? When you look at life with a long-range point of view, you can appreciate how every step you take now influences events in the long run.

There are two kinds of decisions: passive and active. An active decision takes you out of the status quo. It has movement and energy to it, and its consequences are much more controllable than those of a passive decision. A passive decision—a decision by default—is a resignation to let your life be ruled by external circumstances. You tacitly agree to go where the wind blows you. Therefore, paradoxically, by not making a decision, you are, in effect, making a decision. You have opted for inactivity, which also has its consequences. Recall the familiar adage: If you fail to plan, you plan to fail.

Snow skiing instructors have a saying, "You have to move to learn and learn to move." Life is the same way. It's better to make mistakes and learn than to be perfectly inactive.

THE FORMULA FOR GROWTH

There is only one formula for growth and success that works:

Insight + risk + hard work = Growth.

Although this formula makes perfect sense, most people do not live by it. Their equation looks like this:

$$\text{Insight} + \text{no risk/little work} = \text{Enlightened neurosis.}$$

By "enlightened neurosis," we do not mean to diagnose everyone as eccentric. On the contrary, we all have some neurotic behaviors; life would be bland without them. We simply mean that most people spin their wheels and live frustrated lives. They gain some insight—perhaps by watching Phil Donahue—but don't turn those insights into the risks and hard work that culminate in changes. People resist change. You may be enlightened but caught in the cycle that characterizes neurosis: knowing the solution to your problem but not doing anything about it.

This book will make the task of writing articles and books as easy as possible, but you will have to keep up your half of the deal. You have to make the commitment of time and effort. Look around and determine whom you want to emulate. Do you want to be like the people who have procrastinated for years and still have not written their books? Or would you rather knuckle down and have a sense of accomplishment in six months or a year?

Find a Mentor

When you find positive people to emulate, try to develop mentor relationships with them. A support group is extremely important for writers, consultants, speakers, trainers, and other people who have to sell themselves for a living. The group doesn't have to be large, but it does need to be encouraging.

The most powerful encouragement comes from someone you respect; no, make that someone you worship. Find a successful writer, consultant, or CEO and ask to adopt him as a mentor. Buy this person lunch periodically, and tap his knowledge of business, marketing, and anything else that will help you get ahead. There is a great deal to be learned from people who are successful. They are an excellent source of inspiration and motivation. After spending time with your mentor, you will be exhilarated with the vision of what you are striving to be.

Visualization

Visualization is a powerful tool for self-improvement and the achievement of goals. The mind's ability to transfer mental rehearsals into actual behaviors is astounding. Numerous studies on visualization have been conducted in the United States and the Soviet Union. In one of them, Soviet scientists divided their experimental subjects, athletes, into four groups. One group practiced their sport in the usual manner. The second group practiced 75 percent of the time and visualized practicing 25 percent of the time. The third group used a 50-50 ratio of practice and visualization. The fourth group practiced 25 percent and visualized practice 75 percent of the time. The most effective combination for increased athletic performance turned out to be 75 percent visualization and 25 percent practice.

You can use visualization in many ways. If you want to improve your tennis game, practice mentally. Envision yourself doing everything right. If you want to reduce the jitters before giving a presentation, meditate on it. See yourself approaching the podium completely relaxed, delivering a dynamic, informative, entertaining program, and receiving a standing ovation afterward.

Writers, too, can capitalize on the power of visualization. Imagine yourself easily and joyfully writing page after page of high-quality material. See yourself being productive, with the words flowing effortlessly as you complete one article or chapter after another. If you envision the process of writing a book as being easy and pleasurable, you increase the chances that it will be.

The process of visualization dovetails well with the concept of self-image. Simply stated, all the things you think about yourself become your multifaceted self-image. After years of living and thinking, you have a repertoire of mental images of yourself. Some people think they are attractive and act accordingly. Others have an image of being poor and end up living that way, no matter how much money they have. For every character trait, we all have images of ourselves and how we fit those descriptions.

You can use this knowledge to expand your self-image to include being someone who is fully capable of writing a book. No doubt you have heard someone say, "Oh, I could never get in front of a group to speak." Anyone with that attitude can't; that person's self-image has to change to include the belief that he can do it. The same principle applies to writing: Instill in yourself the belief that you can write articles and books. That's not hype; it's the self-assuring truth that you can do it.

For many people, visualization requires as much self-discipline as writing. If you are among them, use an affirmation to give yourself the additional mental thrust.

Affirmations

Another valuable tool for influencing the unconscious mind, especially the self-image, is the use of affirmations, positive sentences that, when repeated to yourself over time, lead to a desired change in attitude.

Use affirmations in relation to writing to boost your confidence and motivation. Write out what you want to accomplish, and then read or say these sentences to yourself several times a day.

State affirmations positively. For example, if you want to overcome procrastination, write, "I am working on my writing projects every day." You should *not* write, "I am not procrastinating." Our minds do not recognize negations. If I tell you, "Don't think of elephants," you'll think of elephants.

Affirmations and visualizations don't have to be true at present but should be written *as if* they were true. Affirmations are things to which you aspire, so they must be achievable. An affirmation such as, "I am giving 100 speeches per year at $5,000 each" is obviously better than "I am growing younger every day." The former you can achieve; the latter would take a miracle or a brilliant biochemist—and if you come up with either, you will give 100 speeches per year at $25,000 each! Our favorite unrealistic affirmation is one of Garry's: "I am omniscient and omnipotent, and soon the world will discover I've returned."

Use the following affirmations to improve your writing habits and skills:

"I am enjoying my writing every day."
"I am making the time to work on my book every weekend."
"I am easily writing three pages per day."

"My mind is lucid, and words come quickly to me."

"My book is doubling the number of consulting jobs I do each year."

Create your own affirmations to suit your needs and dreams, but don't limit them to your professional life. Many people swear that affirmations and visualizations will help you achieve virtually anything. Certainly they are worth the effort.

The Self-image and Personal Change

While growing up, we all had thousands of experiences that caused us to make decisions and draw invalid conclusions. For example, imagine a three-year-old child who tries to help her father wash the car. Not knowing any better, she picks up the steel wool intended for the tires and begins rubbing the paint. Her father, outraged, sends her into the house with tears streaming down her face. The little girl has no idea why she has been treated so badly. In an attempt to understand, she unconsciously comes to some conclusions about life. She may decide helping her father is bad or, worse, concludes that she is a bad person who is not worthy of helping her father.

The cumulative effects of life-long experiences, positive and negative, shape our self-esteem and self-image. That is part of what makes everyone different. Confidence, or the lack of it, is a learned characteristic.

When you confront an idea or behavior inconsistent with your self-image (as you've defined yourself so far), you reject it and close the door to its' becoming a new part of you. Unconsciously you compare the new behavior—good or bad—to your standard repertoire and think, "Forget it; that's not me!"

All this can be undone. With time, experimentation, and practice, you can undo the years of conditioning and add new behaviors to your life. The key is to introduce new behaviors gradually.

A good example is the thought process of someone who habitually says "um" between sentences. He does this to fill the gaps when speaking to a group; he believes silence implies incompetence or ignorance. His self-image thus unrealistically demands that he appear perfectly lucid and knowledgeable at all times. If he is to overcome saying "um," he has to realize the audience will not get up and leave if he pauses to think. His self-image expands to accept the behavior of occasionally being silent. With the pressure of perfectionism off, he stops saying "um" and becomes a better speaker.

OVERCOMING WRITER'S BLOCK

What exactly is writer's block? If you were to ask a half-dozen writers, you would get two dozen answers, and none of them would be wrong. One thing is certain: Writer's block has plagued writers since humans first used sticks to draw marks in the sand.

Ultimately the definition of writer's block is a personal one. Only you know what kind of writer you are. If your pattern is to write sporadically, then you can't consider nonproductive days or weeks as being blocked. If you write every day or aspire to writing every day, an unintentionally unproductive week might be a sign of writer's block.

There are two criteria for determining if you are in the throes of writer's block. The first is sincerity. Ask yourself if you truly want to get some writing done. This question is best asked when you are alone, in case an argument ensues. If your answer is "no," then think of other things to do besides anguishing over your lack of productivity. If your answer is "yes," that is, if you truly intend to work on your article or book but nothing is happening, either you are not putting forth much effort or you are blocked.

Reject Your Fear of Rejection

In examining fear of rejection, the similarity of writing and speaking again becomes apparent. Both require a performance for which you are judged by an audience. In both cases you open yourself up to the possibility of criticism and rejection.

There are many opportunities for writers to be rejected. Editors reject query letters, articles, and books every day. Friends and associates can give negative feedback on something they critiqued. Agents and publishers reject writers regularly.

When your writing is rejected, it is your work that is being rejected, not you. Let's look at this rationally, piece by piece.

When your work is turned down, criticized, rejected, or otherwise treated unkindly, it is one person's opinion, and that opinion should not be given so much weight as to crush you. Opinions are not always valid. There are innumerable stories of people being told they had no talent and would never be successful. Burt Reynolds and Clint Eastwood are two well-known examples. Obviously someone was wrong. The bottom line is that there is no accounting for taste. As Shakespeare wrote, "One man's meat is another man's poison."

The second stumbling block to overcoming a fear of rejection is the notion that you have been rejected as a person. Writers closely identify with and take pride in their work. You should not, however, equate a rejection of your writing with a rejection of yourself. There are plenty of other situations in life in which you can take the rejection personally. Don't do it with your writing. Besides, your writing ability will grow and improve with practice. What you write today may not be an accurate representation of your true ability or future success. If your writing is truly bad, hire someone to transform your ideas into readable copy.

There is another way to look at rejection: It is a fact of life for writers. If you want to write and not risk rejection, self-publish your book and don't ever submit articles to professional journals. That's a safe option but not a wise business move.

The healthiest way to maintain your self-confidence after a rejection is to talk to yourself nicely. You feel what you think. If you think negative thoughts, you will experience negative emotions. Tell yourself that the rejection is not catastrophic and is not worth mental anguish. One rejection is not the final word on you and your writing ability.

Get Outside Support

There are times when people need outside support. This can take the form of counseling or professional associations like the National Speaker's Association (NSA) or the American Society of Training and Development (ASTD). You can find support through writers' groups, your mentor, and friends and family. Anyone who will give you emotional support for your creative aspirations is a valuable resource.

Some writers fall prey to a downward spiral. When they are not productive, they feel bad; the worse they feel, the less they write; the less they write, the worse they feel; and so on. Obviously this spiral must be stopped if you expect ever to complete an article or write your book.

The best writing is done when you are cheerful and optimistic. To avoid the pitfall of the downward spiral, write something—anything—at a set time every day or every other day. Create a routine and write something, even if it needs heavy editing.

Avoidance Rituals Revisited

Your writer's block usually will turn out to be a simple case of cold feet. Many great writers have talked about the rituals they used for avoiding work. Hemingway drank, Dostoyevsky gambled, and Steinbeck was a compulsive letter writer. What do you do? Neatly arrange your shoes in the closet? Wash your laundry even though it's already clean? Eat? Make phone calls and gab? Whatever it is, figure it out and stop doing it. Knowing your avoidance behaviors and your own definition of writer's block will put you in a position to overcome it.

Abandon Your "Shoulds"

"Shoulds" get people in a lot of trouble with themselves. They cause guilt, frustration, and resentment and get in the way of living life with more ease. Guilt and frustration are angry thoughts directed at yourself; resentment is anger directed toward someone else.

A "should" is an expectation that is not fulfilled by yourself or someone else. It is a standard of behavior—perhaps established arbitrarily—that you heard from someone else and that you have not accepted as your own. The frustration comes into play when you become angry at yourself for not doing as you think you "should." Guilt is the same kind of anger, but it refers to the past: "I should have done this or said that." Resentment develops when someone else does not live up to your expectations. Your inability to control or change that person makes you angry.

The best way to rid yourself of "shoulds" is to accept yourself as you are. Stop berating yourself for not living up to the perfect images you have unrealistically concocted for yourself. Forget about perfection. (All the perfect people we know are insufferably boring anyway.) This does not mean you will abandon all your self-improvement goals. It does mean you will work toward them without berating yourself for not having achieved them yet. Not everyone is at the apex of achievement, as if there is one. You can be in a transition or striving toward something others already have attained.

"Shoulds" cripple writers in numerous ways. Some writers get hung up on an expectation of how often they should write, the number of pages they should produce each day, the ease with which the writing process should flow, and so on. These are signs of the neophyte. In the beginning your aspirations are high, but you are unfamiliar with the process of writing, so there is a lot of room for disappointment. The key is to get to know yourself and your pattern of productivity. Once that pattern is established, you can be more realistic about what you wish to accomplish in a given time period.

The only time you should let "shoulds" pressure you is when you are being paid to write and/or have a deadline. The imposition of an external responsibility adds a new dimension to writing. Some people thrive under pressure; others resist it. If being under pressure works well for you, arrange to have that pressure applied. One advantage of collaborating with a co-author is the imposition of deadlines.

Reward Yourself Periodically

To ward off the blues that come with all work and no play, take time out to play. Treat yourself to a movie. Go sailing. Eat decadent desserts. Or do what a lot of people do when the going gets tough: Go shopping. Don't forget to give yourself a rest *and* a pat on the back. You will return to your desk refreshed and ready to be productive.

Day Trips and Vacations

A lot of people who are on prosperity kicks or self-improvement crusades turn themselves into workaholics. Some workaholics, on the other hand, simply use work as a form of identity. It is as if they think, unconsciously, "If I am not working, then who am I?" Writers often fall into this trap.

Writing can be an exhausting job. Thinking and writing for hours is a brain drain. It is critical to let your mind cool off. Don't push yourself to exhaustion. Take days off as the rest of the world manages to. Go for a drive in the mountains or to the ocean. Take a vacation if you can. Travel stimulates your imagination and may give you ideas for future projects. *Do not* work on new ideas while you are away; you need enough time to recharge yourself fully. You can, however, jot the ideas down for consideration when you return.

Write Something Else

When you become bogged down on a project, clear your mind by working on something else—something unrelated to your project or simply another aspect of the same project. Instead of writing, bring a fresh perspective to outlining a chapter or article. Do research at the library. Collect the illustrations and photographs that you will need later. Work on a proposal.

Another alternative to grinding away at a project that is boring you is to write a letter to a friend. If you have no friends or they are tired of your letters, write to us. Your letters will probably be the only fan mail we receive. The digression will serve you well.

Try to get dried-up creative juices flowing again by writing something descriptive. Choose a person, a picture, a place, or an event and describe it. You don't even have to write complete sentences. Use the technique known as free association if you wish. Brief phrases will do. For example, Garry once wrote, "Curvaceous, seductive, compelling, lofty, cool, and waiting to be conquered" while looking at a picture of a snow-covered mountain.

Read an Encyclopedia

If you are stuck in a mode where all you can do is hurl "shoulds" at yourself, relax, pick up a reference book, and thumb through it. An encyclopedia, a book of quotations, a thesaurus, a dictionary, or Strunk and White's *The Elements of Style* are terrific diversions. The material will stimulate your cerebral cortex far better than television.

Start a Hobby; Meet New People

Stimulating your mind in one area can improve it in others. If you have writer's block, meeting new people or taking up a hobby may break you loose. Go to a nightclub or a party, and talk to others about your book. Talking about it may get you excited again. In these situations, you never know what you will pick up to work with. People are the best sources for examples, anecdotes, jokes, information, and ideas, and you don't have to worry about plagiarism.

The distraction of a hobby will take your mind off what ails you. Distractions, like vacations, provide the emotional distance that you need to return to your work with more enthusiasm.

Keep a Journal

Some people like to look back to see what they've done, while others prefer to forget. Keeping a journal can give you insight into your thoughts, behaviors, and patterns of productivity. You can look back to see if and when you were blocked and how long it lasted. For example, knowing that you typically become blocked each year around Christmas will prevent you from getting upset when it happens again this year. In fact, you might plan on it, lower your expectations of yourself, and take a vacation from the guilt.

Journals remind you that difficult times can be overcome, as they have in the past. There is some consolation in knowing that time heals all wounds . . . until the next time.

Get Professional Help

Writers tend to be creative and emotional. If writer's block has got you down for an inordinately long time and someone in your support group cannot snap you out of it, seek professional counseling. This does not mean you have to sign a ten-year contract with a psychiatrist and fund his second mortgage. Go as many times as necessary to gain some insight and work out whatever prevents you from being productive. The hands with which you type are inextricably connected to your head. A closer look at what you are thinking is a sure way to free your hands.

There are many ways to end writer's block if you are motivated to do so. The trick is to catch yourself before you get trapped in the downward spiral of feeling bad because you are unproductive and being unproductive because you feel bad. You have to break that cycle if you want to enjoy writing.

If nothing else, it is important to realize you must do something about writer's block. It is not an inevitable part of being a writer but a symptom of other problems and, ultimately, a waste of time.

Giving yourself a psychological advantage is indispensable in any game. It is the element that distinguishes the winners from the losers. Paul Speicher, in his book *The Courage That Comes from Constructive Thinking* (Diction Books, 1986), draws an analogy between seeing and being. If you were locked in a pitch-black room for a long time, your vision would become significantly impaired due to a lack of stimulation to the optic nerve. Think of your mind as a room in which you live for your entire life. If the room is dark, you will not see as well as someone whose room is bright. If you decorate your room with dreary, depressing colors, you will be much less cheerful than someone who chooses stimulating colors. If the pictures on the walls that you look at daily are pictures of past failures and future fears, you will live according to those pictures. They will, metaphorically, blind you to the brighter, more promising pictures that could exist. Better to decorate your room with pictures of past victories and anticipated future successes.

This advice may sound a bit idealistic and simplistic, but it works. The only obstacle to enlisting your mind as your strongest ally is laziness, and we already know what that is.

The hard work that leads to success always begins in your mind. To get to the top, take the time to start at the top.

SMALL STEPS TO SUCCESS

Work to Be Done   **Deadline**

Goal setting

1. If you are unfamiliar with the basics of goal   _____
   setting, go to the library and read some perti-
   nent articles.

2. Write out your short- and long-term goals.   _____

Visualizations and affirmations

3. Think of five new images of yourself that you   _____
   would like to achieve.

4. Write out descriptions of those five images   _____
   and visualize yourself as being them for five
   minutes twice a day. Using positive statements, write as many affirmations as you
   would like.

5. Read these affirmations aloud once after   _____
   breakfast, lunch, and dinner.

Avoiding writer's block

6. Think of seven to ten ways to get away from   _____
   work and enjoy yourself.

7. Buy a notebook and start a journal. Write in   _____
   it for at least ten minutes each night.

Get Started on This List Today

3

TURN YOUR COMMUNICATION SKILLS INTO WRITING SKILLS

Your first priority in writing, as in speaking, is to communicate effectively. If I were to write or say, "If you don't got no good ideas, you ain't gonna be interesting," my message would be destroyed by the words. My reader or listener would be hopelessly distracted by the thought, "This guy's English is terrible. As far as I'm concerned, he has no credibility." And that's as it should be. If you fail to communicate effectively, your credibility should suffer.

As a beginning writer striving to communicate well, it is important for you to strike a balance between grammatical abandonment and obsessive compliance. If you insist on gravitating toward one extreme or the other, choose the compliance end of the continuum. When you address a group of people, no one cringes when you say *gonna*. In a written piece, however, you had better write *going to*, or else people will cringe. Your choice of words reflects your intelligence, which gets back to credibility.

Effective consultants, professional speakers, trainers, and writers deal in the same commodities: information, anecdotes, examples, quotations, statistics, and humor. The difference between speakers and writers is that writers think before writing and speakers think before speaking (well, sometimes). The thought processes are similar. In effect, a writer speaks to readers. Words should ebb and flow as they do when you speak.

The basic ingredients of a written piece, speech, or training program are all the same; they are ingredients of communication.

INFORMATION

We have all had the unpleasant experience of listening to a college professor, lecturer, or instructor who left us feeling that nothing worthwhile was said. The speaker danced around his subject and added bits of humor, anecdotes, and quotations but never gave us anything concrete to take home and use. The message was more fluff than meat.

As you embark on your book project, one of your first tasks is to determine if you have enough meat for the book. There are far too many books that should have been reduced to a series of tight, informative articles. Here we'll assume you have enough information to fill a book. Now you have to know the best way to present your material. The three keys to imparting your knowledge successfully are to make the information factual, specific, and useful.

Factual Information

Facts and figures are indispensable to any written or verbal presentation. Beginning writers tend to omit hard facts because digging them out can be time-consuming, and some writers find facts difficult or boring to write about. It is much more fun and creative to wax poetic or craft a brilliant metaphor than to cite statistics. Solid information, however, connects your subject to reality and makes it memorable.

Present information in a way that builds your image as an expert. Anyone can write, "Pesticides are a danger to your health." It carries more weight, however, to say, "In 1955, approximately 300 million pounds of DDT smothered our growing foods and killed every bug and animal it touched. Since then, the problem has only gotten worse." That sentence has more impact and shows you did your homework. Experts do a lot of homework. Don't be lazy.

Opinions

As paradoxical as it may be, nonfiction is not always factual; many works are primarily the opinions of the authors. This book is an example of two authors' opinions on writing and marketing books and articles. Our opinions are implied, so it is not necessary to preface everything with, "In our opinion . . ."

Some subjects, however, require special handling to preserve accuracy and avoid ambiguity. If you are writing about the financial world, you should either quote experts or, if you are the expert, back up your statements with proof. For example, don't write, "The economic outlook for the United States is much brighter than most people believe." Instead write, "The economic outlook for the third and fourth quarters of 1992 is steady, if not bright. Interest rates should hold steady or decline due to the sluggish gross national product, new housing starts will increase this summer, and unemployment figures are down by three-tenths of a percent."

Specific Information

Experts back up their opinions with proof. It's fun to philosophize, but complement your brilliance with concrete examples. The speaker who beats around the bush, never hitting the nail on the head, is guilty of overusing fluffy generalizations and clichés. True wisdom lies in giving your audience or readers something worthwhile that will change their lives. This can only be done if you speak and write prescriptively rather than descriptively.

Specific writing is captivating; it holds the reader's attention and makes your point more salient. Which of the following sentences would you rather read: "Tony Alessandra's marketing strategy has helped him publish many articles" or "In the last three years, Tony Alessandra's marketing strategy helped him publish over 350 articles"?

After you have written the first draft of a chapter, go back and highlight words and paragraphs that seem vague. Ask a friend to read your work and point out areas that need more detail. Then do the research to make your work interesting. In the long run, this extra work will give you a higher-quality book or article.

Useful Information

Think back to the ineffective speaker who doesn't give you a worthwhile message. Writers can avoid being accused of this sin by offering useful information—information that allows readers to do something after reading your article. For example, after you have read this book, you will be able to motivate yourself, outline articles and chapters, brainstorm, write a book proposal, write a query letter, write books and articles, edit your work, improve your writing style, understand book contracts, find a collaborator, and market your work.

Providing useful information requires effort on your part. It's easy to write something vague like, "To reduce stress, go home after work and do something nice for yourself." It takes more thought to write, "After work, go home and take a bath, listen to relaxing music, or do stretching exercises." The former sentence is descriptive; the latter is prescriptive. The best combination is a sentence that is factual, specific, and useful: "To reduce stress, doctors recommend you do some exercise after work; aerobics, swimming, tennis, running, and bicycling are the most healthful. Research has revealed sedentary men over the age of fifty are 77 percent more likely to have heart attacks than those who exercise for twenty minutes three times a week."

HOW TO INFORM AND ENTERTAIN

The best way to present information—in speeches, training programs, books, and articles—is to make it convincing and entertaining. To educate, entertain, and motivate, include anecdotes, statistics, examples, analogies, and quotations.

Anecdotes

A short, colorful anecdote is one of the most compelling ways to begin an article. Humorous, pithy little stories are great reader pleasers and can serve as instructive digressions that illustrate your point. Anecdotes make your material interesting by giving the reader a change of pace. They can sugarcoat messages or drive home a point with understatement. Longer anecdotes are acceptable if the payoff is worth it. An example is the following story—perhaps a rumor—that Garry uses in his writing workshops.

A timid, naive, and not very well-traveled woman went to Los Angeles for a seminar on assertiveness training. She was nervous about driving to the big city. When she arrived at her hotel, she took every precaution. She parked in a well-lighted area of the parking lot and locked anything that could be stolen in the trunk. Then she checked into the hotel and headed for her room. She was the only person in the elevator. The door began to close and then suddenly opened to allow three black men, two of whom were rather large, to get in. Nervously, she stood in the corner and stared at the floor. As soon as the door closed, one of the men said, "Hit the floor!" Without thinking, she threw herself spread-eagle on the floor! The men burst into laughter. He had meant, hit the button of *their* floor. She realized what they had meant, got up, brushed herself off, and again stood staring at the floor. When the door opened, she slinked out and walked down the hall to her room. The men kept the elevator door open long enough to see which room was hers. Fifteen minutes later, there was a knock on her door. A delivery boy handed her a beautiful flower arrangement with a note that said, "Thanks for the best laugh I've had in years," signed Eddie Murphy.

Not all anecdotes will fit perfectly into your article or chapter topic. Actual events may need to be tailored to sound good on paper. Sometimes a story should be trimmed, compressed, or exaggerated a little to make it work. Keep in mind that although the specific details of the story can be changed, the overall truth must remain intact. Readers can sense a fabricated story. If your anecdotes fail to ring true, people will lose confidence in you. Besides, we all know truth is stranger than fiction.

For a source of anecdotes, draw on your life and those of people you know well. Try to remember stories you've heard other people tell. Get into the habit of writing down anecdotes you hear to use in the future. Borrowing stories from others is acceptable as long as you give credit. For example, Gene Perret, a professional speaker and former writer for Bob Hope, Phyllis Diller, and other comedians, tells a story about going to the airport with Bob Hope to pick up Hope's wife. They drove onto the end of the runway of the Burbank airport and parked near the chartered jet that had just arrived with Mrs. Hope. Walking down the stairs were a half-dozen priests and then Mrs. Hope. Bob Hope turned to Perret and said, "Why doesn't she just get flight insurance like everyone else?"

It pays to listen—even eavesdrop—to discover new anecdotes. Go to parties and take notes.

Statistics

Statistics impress readers, but don't overdo it. Too many statistics will put your readers to sleep, which is acceptable only if your book is about overcoming insomnia.

Your subject matter will dictate the types and frequency of statistics. In this book, statistics play a limited role. Our readers don't care if 50 percent of all writers experience writer's block during their careers.

It is essential to know who your readers will be. If your subject is academic, statistics are required. Professors, engineers, scientists, doctors, and other left-brain thinkers thrive on data.

Examples

It comes as no surprise that examples are used to back up statements. They flesh out ideas and help readers relate to concepts. You'd be surprised how many writers leave them out. Compare the following two sentences: "Writers and consultants are like cousins; both are in the family of communicators who use words and ideas as the tools of their trade." "Writers and speakers are like cousins."

The first sentence also illustrates one way to give an example without saying *for example*, which is important when you use a lot of examples. Use finesse and a variety of styles. Avoid the awkward phrase, "An example of this is . . ." Don't overwork *for example* or *for instance*. You can include examples without pointing to them; your readers will understand. If you must say *for example*, try putting it in the middle of a sentence: "One of the many values of editing, for example, will be restructuring sentences so they read smoothly."

A few punctuation tips regarding *for example* are in order. When the phrase begins a sentence, it is followed by a comma. When it is in the middle of a sentence, it is surrounded by commas. Substituting *such as* is acceptable but only in the middle of a sentence. When using *for example*, do not follow it with a colon if it introduces a complete sentence; use a colon only when preceding a list. *Such as* does not need a colon before a list: "For example, when you give a speech, you will know your audience is bored if they exhibit behaviors such as snoring, counting ceiling tiles, throwing frisbees, or setting up a volleyball net and choosing sides.''

Analogies

An analogy is a powerful form of an example because it stimulates your readers' gray matter. Showing the similarity between the unfamiliar and the familiar is an excellent way to make your concepts clear. Analogies get your reader involved and allow you to flex your humor muscles.

Analogies can be geared toward your audience. If you are writing for engineers, use mechanical analogies. For men, sports analogies work well. If you are writing for women, use an analogy that only women can truly relate to, such as, ''Writing my first book was as trying as a ten-month pregnancy.''

Quotations

When you say something that can be corroborated by an expert or celebrity, using quotations will make your case even stronger. Quotations enliven your writing and help its readability. In a sense, they say, ''Don't take my word for this; read what so and so has said.''

A quotation should always add information, not repeat it. In your text, if you say snow is white, don't follow up with a quotation from a meteorologist saying, ''Yes, I've observed snow is white.'' That's boring. Your expert's quotation should elaborate on your information. A good quotation for the snowflake example would mention the crystalline structure, light reflection, or whatever the technical reason is for snow's being white.

Don't overuse quotations. Too many make your book or article sound as if you have no ideas of your own. Overuse can cause the reader to ask, ''So what! What is *your* point of view?'' Use quotations sparingly, as you do statistics, anecdotes, examples, and salt.

''Live'' quotations, that is, ones you obtain directly from the person you are quoting, are best if you can get an interview with someone noteworthy. Celebrities and authorities are usually too busy to grant interviews to unknown writers. If you are writing a book, try to get the big shots. Pull whatever strings you have and use all the chutzpah you can muster to get those telephone or in-person interviews. If all else fails, use previously published quotations.

The legal aspect of lifting quotations from books and articles is, not surprisingly, complicated. Distilled to its simplest form, the law allows you to copy quotations without the permission of the copyright owner (usually the author) if your use of the material is reasonable and not harmful to the rights of the copyright owner.

The word *reasonable* concerns quantity, not quality. As long as you don't become greedy, no one will complain. "Not harmful to the rights of the copyright owner" simply means you are not depriving that person of more income. If you copy so many quotations from a book that your own book or article could conceivably hurt the sales of that other person's book, you are infringing on the author's copyright.

This explanation is a legal way of saying, Don't worry about it as long as you do it ethically and in moderation. Simply use quotations to illustrate your own points. The decent thing to do, of course, is to give credit to the source in the text, in a footnote, or at the end of the book in a bibliography.

GRAMMAR

Don't worry. This is not a lengthy discussion of grammar and word usage. We know whom we are dealing with. One advantage that consultants, speakers, and trainers have over other beginning writers is that most already know how to communicate well.

Writing is as much an auditory skill as it is a verbal and an intellectual skill. As you write and later read your work, listen to the words. Use your well-trained ear to avoid the most common grammatical foibles. Leave the nitpicking to editors and spouses. Chapter 14 is devoted to improving your style of writing. Style is as important as proper grammar. An effective and pleasant style will help sell your work. Good grammar simply makes it readable.

Knowing the rules of grammar is not merely a matter of book learning. It is not knowing the names for the parts of sentences. It is not remembering the rules you learned in high school. It is simply tuning in to the sound of what you hear and knowing, more or less intuitively, if it is correct. Most of you know when a grammatical mistake has been made because you've been brung up right and have listened to English being talked correctly most of your life. For most of us, correct English is deeply ingrained.

This is one way that consultants, speakers, and writers are similar. Writers "listen" to their words and sentences in the same way speakers monitor themselves as they speak. Few writers remember the word *ring* is one of the 200 irregular verbs that take an odd form in the past tense. But if you were to say, "The phone ringed yesterday," we would all cringe.

As you read and edit your work, listen to the words and sentence constructions. Your trained ear and the following discussion of common mistakes will take you far in editing your own work.

Common Mistakes in Grammar and Word Usage

Affect/Effect   All you need to know is the difference between a noun and a verb. *Affect* is a verb 99 percent of the time. *Effect* is a noun 90 percent of the time. Knowing this, you would be correct 94.5 percent of the time. (Are you engineers enjoying this?) The exceptions are these: *Affect* is a noun when it is used as a psychological term meaning "emotion" or "feeling"; *effect* can be a verb that means "to cause or bring about." The following examples should clarify:

> *Most common:* "The special effects [fireworks] were the highlight of the evening."
>
> *Most common:* "A standing ovation affects even the most humble actor."
>
> *Less common:* "Doctor, how is chemotherapy going to effect a change ["bring about"] in his thinking and improve his affect ["emotions"]?"

If you find *affect* and *effect* to be difficult words to master, memorize their definitions and be done with it.

Who/Whom   Here's a trick that will make the distinction between these two words simple. To check your *who/whom* usage, substitute *he* for *who* and *him* for *whom*; then rewrite the phrase in question form to see how it sounds.

"John Thompson is the consultant who wrote the best-seller, *Postponing Procrastination*. With the substitution it becomes, "He wrote the best-seller . . ." not "Him wrote the best-seller . . ."

"Steve Wright is the author whom they selected to speak." Rewritten, it is, "They selected him to speak."

At the beginning of a question, *who* is always used instead of *whom*, which is stilted and outdated. "Who are you trying to impress by saying *whom*?"

There are many other pronouns to become comfortable with—*he/him, she/her, we/us*, and *I/me*. Rather than explain them all and risk boring you, we highly recommend that you refer to Strunk and White's *The Elements of Style* when you have a question on word usage. You will find it helpful and discover that it is correct to say, "This is a good reference book for you and *me*."

Which/That *That* is a defining pronoun. It specifies something about the subject of your sentence: "The computer that you are looking for is on her desk." The phrase starting with *that* leads you in the direction of a specific computer. For the purpose of describing which computer is the one of interest, the phrase cannot be eliminated from the sentence.

Which adds information and begins phrases that are helpful but not essential to the sentence: "The fastest computer, which I love to use, is on her desk."

Another way to determine whether to use *which* or *that* is to listen carefully and determine whether the phrase can be enclosed in parentheses. If it can be, use *which*; otherwise use *that*. For example, "You could, if you wanted to break up your writing with digressions (*which* slow down the reader), enclose your "which" phrases in parentheses. This is, however, a tiresome practice *that* should be avoided."

That is commonly overused. If you use a word processor, after you have finished an article or chapter, go back over it with a global search and delete every superfluous *that*. If you are not sure, ask yourself if the meaning of the sentence will change if *that* is deleted. If it will not, take it out. In the following statement, *that* should be deleted: "I'm sure that you will find your writing will sound more professional if you follow my advice."

That and *who* are often confused. *That* qualifies inanimate objects; *who* describes people. "The person *that* ran for Congress had many supporters" may sound correct because of common misusage; however, "the person *who* . . ." is the correct form.

Its/It's This is an easy one to remember. *It's* is a contraction of *it is*. If you can say "it is" instead of "it's," use an apostrophe. *Its* is a possessive pronoun. Something always belongs to it or is its possession. "What is it? It's a dog that loves to chase its tail."

Their/They're/There You may have to memorize the meanings, spellings, and usage of most homonyms. Unfortunately, there are few tricks for differentiating homonyms, so just memorize them. For these three:

Their is a possessive pronoun: "Dogs love to chase *their* tails."

They're is a conjunction of "they are." "*They're* going to get fur in *their* mouths (the dogs, that is)."

There is a location in time or space. "*There* once was a time when people put their belongings over *there* [in that corner]."

However *However* means "nevertheless," "yet," or "in spite of that." It is most often used as a conjunction in the middle of a sentence: "It's a dog-eat-dog world out there; however, you shouldn't let the competition discourage you."

However can be the first word of a sentence, but it will not mean "nevertheless"; it will mean "to whatever extent" or "no matter how (much/far)"—for example, "However discouraging the odds, he never gave up." "However you plan to do it, I wish you luck."

Lie/Lay When Bob Dylan sang, "Lay, lady, lay. Lay across my big brass bed," he was grammatically out of tune. He should have sung, "Lie across my big brass bed." Of course, creative license picks up where grammatical fidelity ends.

The word *lay* requires an object as in, "I'm going to lay *you* down across my big brass bed" or "I'm going to lay *this tray* down and give you breakfast in bed." The past tense would be, "Yesterday you *laid* across my big brass bed."

Lie does not take an object. You can say, "I'm going to lie down." The only time you can use *lay* in the present tense is when there is an object. Of course, you could create a twist in usage and say, "I'm going to *lay myself* [the object] down on the bed and get a good night's rest."

The past tense is where all the trouble begins—as if you're not confused enough already. *Lay* is also the past tense of *lie*. Bob Dylan would have been correct if he had said, "Yesterday, she lay across my big brass bed." If she were still there today, Bob might want to go lie with her. The key is that when you use *lay* without an object, make sure you are talking about the past tense of reclining.

Pronouns That Disagree

Pronouns have to be in the same number—singular or plural—as the nouns to which they refer. The most common mistake is the use of a singular noun with a plural pronoun, as in "The women's basketball team *are* having *their* best season since 1983." Wrong. Although the team has many members, the entity "team" is singular. The sentence should read, "The women's basketball team *is* having *its* best season since 1983."

There is a new trend developing in which writers attempt to avoid the gender problem; that is, they need to choose between *he* and *she* all the time. You've probably heard people say things like, "I had a friend over for dinner last night. *They* brought a bottle of wine." It should be, "*He* [or *she*] brought a bottle of wine." Regardless of the motive, it is awkward and confusing to use the words *they* and *their* in place of *he* or *she* and *his* or *her*. For a more detailed discussion, see "The Degenderization of Language" in Chapter 14.

Verbs That Disagree

When you put two nouns together, it often sounds as if the verb should be singular—for example, "Hard work and dedication *helps* me succeed." No, they don't. "Hard work and dedication *help* you succeed."

When you run across the conjunction *and*, check to see if it forms a compound subject—phrases like "You and I" and "Jack and Jill." If you find a compound subject, make sure the verb after it is plural. "Bonnie and Clyde *are* on the run," not "*is* on the run."

There are some exceptions to this rule. Certain clichés are so inseparable they are considered to be a single entity, as in "bread and butter," "give and take," and "salt and pepper." It's proper to say, "Bread and butter is what I eat for breakfast, and salt and pepper is what I put on it."

Misplaced Modifiers

Misplaced modifiers—sounds like a group of behavioral psychologists who are lost. A misplaced modifier is a written optical illusion that confuses the reader. For example, "The record features Dylan singing to a child that is scratched." We know *scratched* refers to the record, not the child, but the construction is awkward, misleading, and distracting. The way to avoid these constructions is to keep related words together. Don't get fancy; instead say, "The scratched record features Dylan singing to a child."

HOW TO WRITE GOOD

In his book, *Fumble-Rules* (Doubleday, 1990), William Safire takes a lighthearted look at grammar and usage. The following partial list of chapter titles from his book will bring a smile to your face. They not only introduce the chapter's contents but also exemplify the broken rules. If you do not understand the errors illustrated in the following sentences, get his book. On second thought, get it anyway.

A writer must not shift your point of view.
Don't use Capital letters without good REASON.
If I've told you once, I've told you a thousand times; resist hyperbole.
Avoid commas, that are not necessary.
Verbs has to agree with their subjects.
Writing carefully, dangling participles should be avoided.
Never use a long word when a diminutive one will do.
Use parallel structure when you write and in speaking.
You should just avoid confusing readers with misplaced modifiers.
Don't verb nouns.
"Avoid overuse of 'quotation "marks." "
Never, ever use repetitive redundancies.
Last but not least, avoid clichés like the plague.

Strive to write clearly and effectively. Mastering the basics of grammar and usage is like learning the scales of a musical instrument. You don't have to know them well to play a song, but the more you know, the further you can go as a musician. And the more you know about theory, the greater your freedom of expression will be when you want to jazz around with the scales.

Excellent writing is rarely accomplished in the first draft. Writing is a discipline of rewriting, editing, shaping, sculpting, and perfecting the expression of thoughts on paper. Editing is similar to refining a recipe. After tasting the first batch, you decide what is needed—more of this, less of that. If you've ever made spaghetti sauce, you know sugar, in moderation, reduces the bitterness. Too much sugar, however, ruins it. Words are the same way. Adjectives add spice to your nouns, but too many make your writing too sweet and ruin it.

SMALL STEPS TO SUCCESS

Work to Be Done   **Deadline**

1. Buy a copy of *Elements of Style*, and read it.   _____
2. Reread and study this chapter.   _____
3. Write two anecdotes related to some aspect   _____
   of your field.
4. Write an example using statistics as they re-   _____
   late to your field.
5. Construct an analogy for two aspects of your   _____
   field.
6. Find quotations that pertain to your topic.   _____
7. Write sentences using the words explained in   _____
   the grammar section of this chapter.
8. Read a good book to develop your ear for   _____
   proper language.

Get Started on This List Today

PART TWO

Start With Articles

4

THE EASY WAY TO WRITE ARTICLES

Although this book was written with the goal of helping you write and publish a book, an important step in this process—indeed, a worthwhile career step in its own right—is the writing of articles for periodicals. There are two main benefits to publishing articles before setting off on a book project. The first is that book publishing editors often look for previous writing—or "clips"—before seriously considering a book proposal. Unless you are Lee Iacocca, editors usually want some evidence that the business world values what you have to say. The addition of clips in your proposal also reassures editors as to your ability to write for publication. Although there are no hard-and-fast rules, your chances of obtaining a book contract rise enormously with the number and variety of articles under your belt.

Second, writing articles helps you hone your writing skills and prepares you for the task of book writing. Once you know you can write a tight article, you can be sure that a book chapter won't hold any surprises for you. If you can write a short article, you only need a longer outline and a bit more information to write a chapter. For this reason, keep in mind that most of the principles for *book* writing are also contained in the following chapters on writing for articles.

The next four chapters of *Publish and Flourish—A Consultant's Guide* focus on getting you up to steam with article writing. We begin the process in this chapter with guidelines for putting an article together. This chapter will help you come up with your core ideas and point you on the way to writing a readable piece. Before you begin writing, however, be sure you read Chapter 5 on positioning and selling your work. You'll want to get a sense of your market— and how you'll *approach* your market—before you start. You'll face some important decisions like whether to approach newsletters, trade magazines, or more mainstream publications. Your decisions will greatly affect the kind of article you'll eventually write.

FOCUS YOUR THEME

Every book, article, chapter, poem, love letter, even a grocery list, needs a theme. The theme is what you are going to write about and accomplish in your piece. The theme of an article might be as general as "ways to increase sales productivity" or as specific as "improving telephone skills for cold calling." Keep in mind that the more specific your theme is, the easier it will be to write an article or chapter.

After you have defined your theme, ask yourself all the logical questions that pertain to the subject. Brainstorm these questions by clustering (to be covered later), and then arrange them in a linear, logical order. If all are important, each question could be a major section of the chapter or article.

An example of a theme and its accompanying questions is, "The Use of Relationship Strategies to Increase Sales." Some questions to be answered in the article would be:

- What is the premise of relationship strategies?
- How does it relate to the sales situation?
- What can it do for the reader/salesperson?
- Is it easy to learn?
- What are the specific strategies?
- What are some examples of relationship strategies in the workplace?

Although book chapters and articles both require a theme, keep in mind that articles require something extra. With any short-form written piece, you must hook your reader quickly. A hook creates a sense of relevance and urgency in the reader's mind and motivates him to read it now. A book chapter does not have to sell the reader. It is read as part of the larger work that has already been sold to the reader.

Articles written by business people fall into three general categories: theoretical, case histories, and how-to or advice. Articles written strictly in the abstract are more appropriate for academic and upper-level management readers. Everyone can relate to case histories and how-to articles, which makes them far more salable. The combination of case histories and how-to is very strong; the case history conveys to the reader, "Here are people who had the same problem you have, and here's how they solved it." The how-to gives readers specific advice on how to solve the problem.

HOW TO OUTLINE YOUR ARTICLE

You will use outlines in many phases of writing. When you first think of your idea, outline it to see if you have enough material for a book. Later, outline chapters and articles so you will know exactly what each will contain. There are two basic ways to outline an idea; each is appropriate at different times.

Clustering

The clustering method of outlining (some people call it "mind mapping") is the best overall tool for brainstorming the contents of a book, chapter, or article. It allows you to list your ideas, and it stimulates creative thinking. By free associating, you quickly and easily generate new ideas. Unlike vertical or traditional outlining, clustering is a nonlinear process that has no beginning or end.

To outline by clustering, write the name of the subject in the middle of a page and circle the word or words. As ideas come up, draw spokes out from the circle, and write key words by those spokes. Move around the circle with new ideas, and extend out from existing ideas, as illustrated in Figure 4.1.

The advantage of clustering is that it does not limit you to logical, sequential thinking as vertical outlining does. The freedom

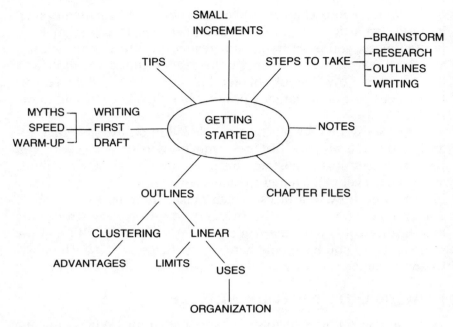

Figure 4.1   Clustering

to contemplate any idea at any time loosens your thinking and helps you brainstorm. Linear outlines, on the other hand, confine you to thinking about one subject at a time as you progress down the page. You may feel uncomfortable jumping from subject to subject when using a linear outline, but clustering encourages it.

Clustering is helpful when you are developing the major concepts to be covered in your article or chapter and while writing. If you find yourself at a loss for ideas, take a fresh piece of paper and cluster the theme you are writing about. Include the ideas you've already covered, and you will find new ones surfacing, no doubt donated by your muse.

Traditional Outlines

Traditional outlines that list titles, subtopics, and details in a vertical fashion are appropriate when you must see the order of things. Obviously the contents page of a book would look ridiculous in clustered form. Traditional outlines are helpful after you have clustered your ideas. Before writing the first draft of an article or chapter, rearrange the clustered outline into linear form so you will know the order of subtopics. Another method is to number the different parts of the clustered outline and follow that sequence in writing.

A traditional outline should have at least three supporting details per subtopic:

Working Title
I. Subtopic
   A. Detail
   B. Detail
   C. Detail
II. Subtopic
   A. Detail
      1. Example
      2. Statistic
   B. Detail
   C. Detail
   (etc.)

There are many ways to organize a book, chapter, or article. The nature of your subject will dictate the most logical way. Here are some choices:

Chronological Order
In the order something was seen or done.
In the order something should be seen or done.
In the order from cause to effect.

From General to Specific
From general topic to subtopics and examples.
From theoretical to practical application.
From generalizations to specific examples.

From Least to Most
Easiest to most difficult.
Smallest to largest.

Worst to best or weakest to strongest.

Least important to most important.

Least complicated to most complicated.

Least effective to most effective.

Least popular to most popular.

Giving Both Sides

Pros and cons.

Similarities and differences (compare and contrast).

Assets and liabilities.

Advantages and disadvantages.

The importance of outlines cannot be overemphasized. Writing extemporaneously is unorganized and amateurish. It is better to know exactly where you are going and prepare to go there. In the same way you would present a program or consult with a client only after you have prepared a game plan, so, too, the best writing is produced when there is a structure to follow.

THE OPENING

After you know your theme and the general content to be covered, work on the opening. The best way to write the opening of an article is to answer implicitly the three most important questions in a reader's mind: What is the article about? Why is the subject important to me? Why should I read it now?

To answer these questions, *write out* the answers; do not merely do this exercise mentally. Next, use one of the following opening styles to write your lead.

Quotations

A powerful or amusing quotation can prove effective. If possible, quote someone you interviewed for the article; otherwise quote a celebrity or a well-known expert whose comments pertain to the theme of the article. If all else fails, you may be able to find something useful in a book of quotations. W. Somerset Maugham advised in *The Summing Up* (1938), "It has been said that good prose should resemble the conversation of a well-bred man."

Anecdotes

Anecdotes, like quotations, must be pithy, short, and related to the theme of the article. Never tell a story that leads the reader astray, only to follow it with, "Just kidding; on the serious side . . ." unless you thrive on alienating editors.

One of our favorite anecdotes—not relevant to this discussion, but it proves the power of a great anecdote—is a story about Groucho Marx. During his stint as the host of "You Bet Your Life," Groucho interviewed a woman named Mrs. Story, who had given birth to twenty-two children. "I love my husband," Mrs. Story said enthusiastically. "I like my cigar, too," said Groucho, "but I take it out once in a while."

Philosophical Inspiration

If your opening statement is a generalization or a philosophical treatise, make sure it will grab readers, as this philosophical introduction to an article on time management did:

> Time is nature's greatest force. Nothing can stop it, nothing can alter it. Unlike the wind, it cannot be felt. Unlike the sun, it cannot be seen. Yet, of all nature's forces, time has the most profound effect on us. Time remains constant, but our perception of it changes. When we focus on it, it slows down. When we turn our backs on it, it speeds up. Our illusion makes us think it is something tangible. We arrange it, divide it up, give some to our friends. Sometimes we feel it is precious, at other times we waste it. We give it the power to heal when we say, "Time heals all wounds." It can also kill when we live stressful lives because we "never have enough time." On a day-to-day basis, nothing is defined and redefined in our minds as much as time. It's a wonder we can still recognize it.*

The Unexpected

Creative openings hook the reader, but make sure you know what you are doing and tie it into the theme of the article. A descriptive opening sets the mood, as you can see in D. Keith Mano's introduc-

---

*This introduction to time management, written by Garry Schaeffer, appeared in *The Business of Selling* by Dr. Tony Alessandra and Jim Cathcart (Reston, 1984).

tion to his article on Street Smarts that appeared in *Playboy* Magazine: "We are all game: venison in the streets. A carrion bird has been circling over Central Park. Expect it, *goombah*: everyone loves a good loser. When you leave home, say aloud, Today I'm gonna get rolled, ripped, sharked, gouged, gonged, japped, poached, taken off."*

Achieving that kind of creativity does not happen overnight. It takes, among other things, total immersion in your subject, a command of the language—in this case, street slang—and the ability to wax metaphoric at will.

Experiment with creative openings. Pretend you are writing an article on business travel; describe losing your luggage. Try writing it several ways: seriously, playfully, and sarcastically.

Problems

Consultants are hired to solve problems, so the easiest introduction may be a general description of a problem. Keep it broad; specifics can be filled in later. Remember, the purpose of the introduction is to hook the reader with something to which he can relate or about which he may be curious. You could pose a problem like this: "You've just been promoted to sales manager. You have paperwork, sales meetings, phone calls, fieldwork, training sessions, sales presentations, and a thousand other new responsibilities. Getting organized seems to be the most difficult task. How are you going to do it?"

Questions

Posing questions is more effective in speeches than in writing articles, but many writers like this style. Some start their articles with a series of questions. If you choose this opening, don't overdo it. One or two questions is acceptable; more than three is a nuisance to readers.

The best way to open with a question is to write one that's cogent, such as, "Of all the skills necessary to be a productive salesperson, which one do you think is the most important: social skills, sales techniques, or product knowledge?"

---

*This creative introduction appeared in D. Keith Mano's article, "Street Smarts," in *Playboy*, July 1982, p. 95.

Juxtaposition

By contrasting two seemingly unrelated facts, you can create an interesting opening: "Joe Smith drives a new BMW, owns a $450,000 house, has a million-dollar stock portfolio, and admits to having an IQ of 83. How did he do it?"

Sensationalism

Shock people, and they'll read your article: "Every day you are growing older. Your hair is falling out; your skin is drying and forming wrinkles; your spine is compressing; your arteries are becoming clogged; and your mind is becoming increasingly dull. But there is a way to fight the inevitable."

Statistics

Unless they open your readers' eyes, statistical openings can be boring. Combine statistics with sensationalism, and you've got something. "By the year 2000, one out of two people will have known someone who has died of AIDS."

Write a Dull Lead

The lead is one of the most difficult sentences to write. If you are at a loss for the first line, forget it. Instead of obsessing over the perfect, clever introduction, simply state the topic, and start writing about it. You can always go back and create the red-hot opening when your imagination is on fire.

THE BODY OF THE ARTICLE

The next part of the article is the body. Start with the first question—What is this article about?—and without actually stating it, answer it. Write as much as you can as quickly as possible on that topic. When you have concluded the section or run out of steam, move on to the next logical subject. The more topics you have, the easier it will be to write. Go from one topic to the next, addressing each in the most informative way you can.

The discussion of any one idea can be as short as a paragraph or as long as several pages. The appropriate length will be dictated by the project and the importance of the idea. For articles, limit your discussion; book chapters allow more elaboration. The length of discussion should be proportionate to the importance of the idea.

Each paragraph must relate to the theme. Similarly, each sentence in it must relate to the thrust of that paragraph. Throughout the body of the article, insert statistics, anecdotes, and quotations when appropriate. As you write, new issues will pop into your mind. Address these as well and, if necessary, later, rearrange the order of your paragraphs as logic dictates.

In book chapters and articles, break the flow of the text and present information with bullets for emphasis. This has the following advantages and looks like this:

• Makes important points stand out.
• Breaks up the monotony of pages of solid words.
• Allows you to list numerous items that would look awkward in text.
• Serves as a memory device to improve readers' retention.

THE LIST ARTICLE AND FORMAT

By far, the easiest type of article to write is the list article. It is ideal for beginners because it is useful, marketable, and easy to write. Like other articles, the list article discusses several points under a single theme. In a regular article, each point is discussed within the narrative of a paragraph. In a list article, the text is broken into lists that discuss points. List articles eliminate the need to create smooth transitions between paragraphs and sections.

List articles are ideal for business topics because they lend themselves to the presentation of useful and problem-solving information. To think up ideas for articles, consider problems you can solve in your area of expertise. Each one is a potential article.

The list format can and should be used in book chapters as well. Using various formats makes the material easier to read and holds readers' attention.

The list article consists of three parts: the introduction and theme, the list, and the conclusion. (In a book chapter, the introduction and conclusion are more elaborate than in an article.)

The Introduction

The introduction should be like any other: It entices readers to keep reading and tells them what to expect. If your title is self-explanatory—"Ten Ways to Grow Bigger Tomatoes" or "Seven Ways to Reduce Stress at Work"—spend less time discussing the theme. When you write a query letter to an editor (to be covered subsequently), don't insult his intelligence by talking about the theme of the article if the title is self-explanatory. Instead, show how your article is different from similar articles that have appeared in the past.

The Body

The list forms the body of the article. Its structure depends on the type of article you are writing. The format may look like the enumerated list that follows.

1. **The Problem-Solving List.** This is the most common list article. It answers the questions presented in the introduction by devoting one item in the list to each solution. In an article on reducing stress at work, you might have the heading, "Lunch Hour Remedies," and discuss the benefits of exercise, relaxation, and meditation during the lunch hour. The heading "Laughter at Work" could cover organizing comic relief coffee breaks, noontime joke sessions, and other laugh-inducing ideas.

2. **The Step-by-Step List.** This style is used for a cookbook approach to disseminating information in which the order of the list is crucial. An article to teach readers how to meditate would list the steps sequentially: first you go to India, then you grow a beard, then you sell your shoes, and so on.

3. **The General Information List.** Some list articles compile information about people, places, companies, and products that are useful to readers. You might be writing an article entitled "Networking Organizations for Women" in your area or "Products That Aid Time Management." For these sorts of articles, mention in the introduction the criteria you used to select the listed information. If you write a "best of" article, as in "The Ten Best Advertising Agencies in Peachtree, Georgia," state why they were chosen and, if possible, rank them.

The Conclusion

Articles and chapters, unlike some speeches, cannot end abruptly with, "Thank you and good night." A brief paragraph should wrap everything up into a neat package. A good conclusion gives the reader a feeling of closure and the satisfaction of having received something of value for the time invested in reading. A book chapter can end with a summary but should also serve as a transition to the next chapter.

The ending shows readers you have finished what you set out to accomplish. The introduction stated your theme and intentions; the body supported and elaborated your claims. The concluding paragraph demonstrates that your train of thought remained on track and arrived at a logical destination, on schedule.

Clearly relate your conclusion to the body of the article. This is not a time to throw in miscellaneous examples or leftovers that should have been included earlier, nor is it the place to start a new train of thought. There are exceptions, of course—articles that conclude by posing unanswered questions and calling for further research. You will probably not write one of those.

Good Conclusions Strive to write conclusions that accomplish at least one of the following objectives:

- Answer the question, "So what?" and drive home the points you have already made.
- Emphasize the important points by restating them briefly.
- Raise an important question and answer it. For example, "What does the future hold?" or "Where do we go from here?"
- Employ a quotation by a well-known personality to support the theme of the article.
- Illustrate the need for a change in attitude or behavior.

These types of conclusions are more often used in articles than book chapters. Articles have to stand on their own, so they need conclusions to create closure. A book chapter is only a part of the whole and does not have to answer the question, "So what?" The last chapter of the book should answer that question.

Bad Conclusions Follow these admonitions when ending a chapter or article:

- Never simply repeat your theme or say, "As you just saw" or "It should be clear to you that . . ." If the reader has already forgotten what you have written, the body of the article or chapter has failed.
- Never give a lifeless summary. You can repeat some points, but don't list every idea you have covered.
- Avoid phrases such as, "In conclusion," "To summarize," or "Last but not least." These are as bad as starting your article with, "I'm going to tell you about . . ."
- Don't preach or bark out orders. Your article should be convincing enough to motivate others. The conclusion can give a subtle push, but avoid heavy-handed statements such as, "Don't sit back and let other people run your life." "Get out there and vote." "Be a concerned citizen. Conserve water and curb your dog."
- Avoid gushing hyperboles and extravagant claims. Don't try to end with a bang. (You should have started with a bang.)
- Never make a point that does not relate to the article theme unless you are writing a series of articles or providing a transition to the next chapter. In these cases, teasing readers with coming attractions will make them look forward to the next article or chapter.

If all of this sounds difficult, don't worry. Not only does it sound more difficult than it truly is, but general practice often deviates from the ideal. For proof, consider your daily newspaper or virtually any book you read. Logical construction is a principle practiced in the breach more than compliance. Nevertheless, you should strive to present your ideas in a logical order, at least until you know enough to abandon logic for the sake of art.

CREATING THE VOICE OF AUTHORITY

Regardless of whether you are writing book chapters or articles, your goal is to be perceived as an expert. It's easy to do if you are willing to research your subject and provide the information in a style that builds confidence. Four kinds of information will increase your credibility: using specific descriptions, properly using industry jargon, giving concrete examples, and stating expert facts.

When experts talk shop, they don't generalize. Wine stewards do not recommend red or white wine; they recommend a Bordeaux or Chardonnay. Give your readers useful information, and build your credibility by being specific.

Every field has its own vernacular. Sailors refer to ropes as "lines" and "sheets." Advertising copywriters refer to written words as "copy," not "text." Surgeons call that dreaded instrument a "scalpel" instead of a "knife." If your field has its own vernacular, use it and, if necessary, define it. Don't worry about sounding pedantic or stilted. There is a difference between using language accurately and using it for show.

Backing up your assertions with actual examples, especially case histories, will make you sound like an authority. The same can be said of expert facts—bits and pieces of extra information that add color and depth to your writing. For example, if you are writing about networking, you could mention, "There is nothing new about the practice, but it was revived and renamed by Jerry Rubin, the former '60s political activist. In 1979, he rented Studio 54, a New York City disco, and threw a party for people to make business connections." This is the type of tangential but interesting information that people remember.

If you are not already an expert in your field, spend some time conducting research before you begin writing. Consult as many sources as possible, and read everything you can. As your knowledge grows, you will form your own opinions and be able to present facts and recommendations as your own, not someone else's.

There is another benefit to having done your homework: It enables you to read other peoples' work and judge whether they are writing objectively or with an inordinate amount of self-promotion (placing more emphasis on selling themselves rather than disseminating ideas and facts).

IT'S WHAT YOU SAY *AND* HOW YOU SAY IT

While extensive research will increase the credibility of your work, certain writing styles will help you deliver your message with impact. Take heed of the tips on style discussed in Chapter 14. Here are more tips on writing with authority.

Cut to the Chase

If your chapter or article solves a problem, simply state the problem and give the answer. Never broadcast your obvious intention with, "In this article I will show you how to . . ." That's amateurish. Instead, present the problem with the assumption that everyone has experienced it. Don't try to cover every possibility by saying, "Some of you may, on occasion, perhaps, experience VDT eye fatigue." Get to the point: "VDT eye strain is a common problem among office workers."

Be Logical

Present your ideas in logical or chronological order—whichever applies. Flashbacks, even in the form of anecdotes, do not work well in nonfiction. If your chapter or article contains a description of a complex task, start with the simplest step and move toward the most difficult. If possible, provide photographs or illustrations for clarification.

Use Short Commands

The short, direct cookbook style comes off well when giving commands: "Chop six medium onions. Cry. Add garlic, olive oil, and basil." Use this style in moderation.

Be Assertive

Write as if you were omniscient. Write with confidence and authority, not with qualifiers and conditional phrases. Diluting the impact of commands with, "perhaps you might consider," "I think," "I suggest," and other tentative phrases makes you sound like a wimp. Stand behind your assertions. Tell people what to do and where to go. Don't worry; most people won't follow your advice. That's why how-to books are perennial best-sellers.

Help Readers Relate

To drive home a point, make it personal by occasionally referring to the reader as "you"—either implicitly or explicitly.

Writing articles is an excellent way to cut your teeth as a writer. Start with short pieces—two to four pages—and work your way up to feature-length articles and eventually book chapters (fifteen to thirty pages). When you have enough material to write ten to twenty long articles (aka chapters), you've got a book (more or less).

SMALL STEPS TO SUCCESS

Work to Be Done   **Deadline**

1. Write five one-sentence synopses of anything   _____
   (e.g., ideas, movies, TV shows).

2. Write two or three seventy-five- to one hun-   _____
   dred-word bios and describe your qualifications, background, education, or relevant life
   experiences.

3. Create three new titles for an article idea or   _____
   presentation.

4. Answer the question, "What problems am I   _____
   able to solve?"

5. Think of some clients who may serve as case   _____
   histories to illustrate Step 4.

6. Based on the answers to Step 4, use clustering   _____
   to brainstorm the contents of three articles;
   one short, one medium, and one long.

7. Set three deadlines for writing the articles out- _____
   lined in Step 6.

Get Started on This List Today

5

HOW TO POSITION AND MARKET YOUR ARTICLES

Your time is valuable, so optimize it. Before you write an article, conduct some market research. Determine the article's salability. Is there a market for it? Which publications reach your target market? Answer these important questions first and you will stack the odds of acceptance in your favor.

POSITIONING

Year after year books and articles are written to satisfy a world full of information gluttons. How is it done? How are writers able to sell a finite amount of information to new markets? They use positioning, a marketing technique that identifies a product's niche and shapes its promotion to its target market. Salespeople do positioning all the time by explaining how a product differs from the competition.

Positioning is used in everyday conversations, as well as advertising. Using an analogy such as, "This computer is the Rolls Royce of IBM compatibles," immediately conveys its position to the buyer.

Avis used a clever strategy when it portrayed itself as the hard-working underdog: "We're number two; we try harder." In fact, Avis was number six or seven when it started that campaign, but the advertising got the point across.

To position an article, clearly and realistically identify the intended audience. Determine a way to differentiate it from similar ones. Draw an analogy between it and something that will form a familiar, favorable image in an editor's mind. The use of status symbols, popular books, movies, and celebrities is effective: "The proposed article is the *One-Minute Manager* of financial planning."

Positioning your article for an editor will improve your ability to sell it. Editors are too busy to analyze the market for every article that crosses their desks. Save them the effort by explaining how your piece fits their publication's guidelines. For example, in your query letter, insert a sentence such as, "This article is written for sales managers in the hotel industry. It can be compared to Mark McCormack's book, *What They Don't Teach You at Harvard Business School.*"

Find a novel approach to your subject, and you will not only sell more articles; you will get more consulting jobs and speaking engagements. Even if your expertise is not unique, your ability to reach a new audience and teach the material effectively will put you far ahead of the pack.

A well-positioned article does not have to be unique; it can complement the competition. If you see an information gap or other shortcoming in the content of a previously published article, query the publisher and offer to write an article that fills the gap and paints a fuller picture.

In your query letter, keep the position statement short. A creative analogy is much better than a detailed explanation. Someone once said that every good idea can be written on the back of a business card. If you quickly communicate your concept to an editor, you will increase your chances of being in an enviable position: that of a published writer.

MARKETING

Effective marketing is the key to success for any business. No matter what you do, you are always selling something. If you don't sell a product, you are selling your services. Placing articles in professional journals will strengthen your ability to sell yourself.

As in outside sales, marketing an article requires you to target a market, research your prospects' needs, make contact with prospects, and follow up until you make the sale. The query letter, which presents your proposal, is an important part of this process. Maintaining a working relationship after the sale is important as well.

Target Markets

Naturally you want to sell your article to a prestigious magazine or business journal. The more prestige, the better is the exposure for you. No doubt you are familiar with many publications in your field. In addition to the most popular ones, there are hundreds of other publications where your work may be welcomed. Here's how to find them.

Most public libraries have a number of useful publications. The *Encyclopedia of Associations* is a directory of every type of association imaginable. It is easy to work with and a good directory with which to start. For each association, the encyclopedia provides the president's name, the association's address and telephone number, the number of members, the number of regional groups, a description of the organization and its goals, its publications and newsletters, and meeting and convention frequency. If you cannot find a copy in your library, contact the Gale Research Company, 1400 Book Tower, Detroit, Michigan 48226.

Newsletters of professional associations are an excellent market for articles. You can find them in *Encyclopedia of Associations* or the *National Directory of Newsletters and Reporting Services*, also published by Gale Research. The *Standard Periodical Directory*, issued by Oxbridge Communications, 183 Madison Avenue, New York, New York 10016, is another valuable resource to help you compile a list of periodicals to sell your articles to. It lists more than 68,000 American and Canadian publications grouped in 230 subject categories.

Writer's Market is an annual publication that lists trade and professional journals and magazines. Although its listings contain more information than other similar directories, it has little information on business and professional journals.

There is even a directory on directories, the *Directory of Directories*.

Use the *Encyclopedia of Associations* or other directories to start targeting your market. Look for publications that cater to the industries for which your article would be relevant. The more you peruse the available resources—including appendix C—the more markets you will find. The number you start with and the amount of time you spend promoting your work are entirely up to you.

Initial Research

Before submitting an article or query letter to an editor, determine if the publication is appropriate for your work. There are a number of ways to determine this. The more issues of the publication you can see, the easier your task will be.

Start with Covers Magazines reveal a lot about their editorial direction and readership by their covers. Professional and technical journals do not; they have a captive audience and need not worry about image.

If you aspire to being published in a magazine, no matter how small, study the covers over a six-month period. Are the article titles on the cover similar to the one you have in mind? Is there a fundamental compatibility here?

Study the Contents The article titles in your target publication will not only tell you the obvious but also the less obvious, such as style and focus. Titles can be straightforward or creative. Subjects can be mainstream or unorthodox. Look for patterns. In a business journal, the articles may be mostly technical, mostly behavioral, or mostly eclectic. The orientation may be sales, service, marketing, economics, or something else.

Look at the Ads For magazines, advertisers make the publication possible. Professional journals are less dependent on advertisers but not completely so. Display ads of all sizes will show you who reads the publication. If you want to sell your article, you have to please the editor and readers.

Read the Monthly Columns and Departments A publication's editorial direction is also revealed in its monthly columns and departments. The editor's column points out what issues are hot and where the publication is headed in the future. The brief tidbits "department" that appears in the beginning of most magazines is an excellent place for you to break in. Read these sections for content and style, and then submit unique and informative fillers for them to use.

Read Feature Articles Read these not only for content but for writing quality, style, length, and structure. Take note of the use of photos, graphics, headings, boxes, and other stylistic devices.

Once you have narrowed your search to a manageable number of publications, you are ready to contact them.

Make Contact

There are two ways to contact an editor: by letter or by telephone. The advantage of a query letter is that you can send it simultaneously to a large number of prospects. If you have a computer, you can send an original, personalized copy instead of a photocopy. It is important to give editors the impression they are special. They will take a dim view of you if they suspect you are running a production line.

Your first contact should be by telephone—a brief call to verify the editor's name, the journal's address, and its policy on accepting outside material. You might say, "Hello. Is this Joe Editor? This is So and So. I'd like to verify some information so I can send you something." Then verify the spelling of the editor's name, the address, and other details. If asked what you are sending, reply you are sending a query and ask if he accepts submissions from freelancers. The reason to ask this question is not to see if the editor does; they all do. Instead, you are subtly broaching the subject of your article. If the editor simply says, "Yes, we accept articles from freelancers," you have the choice of replying, "I'll send you a query" or being straightforward and asking him if he has a minute to hear about your idea.

It may be possible for you to describe your article idea to an editor over the telephone. One disadvantage with telephone pitching is the pressure you will be under to sell your idea quickly and effectively to the editor. If asked about your writing background, you will also have to sell your ability to write a good article. Naturally, you will point out your professional experience and mention your track record as a writer, if you have one.

Pitching by telephone does offer advantages, though, of immediate feedback, increased personal contact, and speed. The best way to sell something is in person; the second best way is by telephone. If you can establish a telephone rapport with the editor, you will quickly become more than merely another writer in his file.

To pitch your idea effectively, have a typewritten synopsis of the article by the telephone. Make it short, and include a positioning statement that applies to the journal's market. Have a personal bio at hand so you can quickly and smoothly list your credentials if asked. When you read the article synopsis and your bio, say the words as if you were speaking extemporaneously so you won't appear to be reading. After a while you will have made so many calls that your sales pitch will become smooth and natural.

Simultaneous Submissions

From a marketing standpoint, it makes little sense to submit your query or article to one publication at a time. That would be like a salesperson waiting to close one sale before making a presentation to another prospect. A reasonable shotgun approach is more efficient and yields better results. This is called simultaneous submission: sending your query to several publications with the hope one will buy it. If one does buy it, you are obligated to tell the others your article is no longer for sale.

There is a danger to the shotgun approach. The prestigious journals want exclusive rights to your work. They also like to think they are the only publication to which you have submitted work. Don't even hint you are approaching other editors, unless you are selling a reprint or offering an industry exclusive. If an editor asks you if you sent your material elsewhere, you must tell the truth. There are ethical and practical considerations here. What if you told the editor you submitted the article only to him and then two weeks later you had to call back to tell him another journal bought your article first. Your name would be MUD with that editor for a long time.

The Follow-up

After a positive response to an initial contact, follow up with a cover letter and the query or article, including a bio. Mail this material quickly so they'll be received while your name is still fresh in the editor's mind.

Presenting the Proposal: The Query Letter

The query letter has several purposes. From your standpoint, it is a way to sell your article idea before you write it, thus saving time and money. From an editor's point of view, queries are much faster to read than entire articles. Editors prefer queries initially. If they accept them, they can have a hand in shaping the articles. Editors often hesitate to ask a writer to revise an article but are not reluctant to suggest a new slant before it is written.

Sending query letters allows you to market your articles before you write them. You will be able to submit more article ideas to more journals and magazines, reduce research time, receive faster replies from editors, and spend time writing only those articles for which you have commitments.

Queries are used for all types of articles except those of a thousand words (four pages) or less. Short articles, which can be read quickly, should be submitted in finished form.

The One-sentence Synopsis When writing a query, quickly and succinctly convince an editor that you have an interesting, well-focused idea and the expertise to write the article. Outline your idea completely so there are no gaps in your vision of the material. Then imagine yourself describing the article to a friend in a brief telegram. This is an important step. In a sentence or two, you should be able to convey the essence of your topic and how it will benefit readers.

One way to learn the art of synopsis writing is to study *TV Guide*. Movies always have one-line descriptions, such as, "When a man commits suicide, his closest friends from college gather for the funeral and reflect on how their lives have changed since the 1960s" (*The Big Chill*). After you have read some of these descriptions and see the basic concept, practice writing them for books you've read, movies you've seen, people you know. Finally, write a synopsis for every topic on which you speak, train, or consult.

If you're going to write an article on a subject that has been around for a while, give it a new twist. The areas of time management, networking, and stress reduction are some of the many topics that are well worn but still relevant. A truly unique slant will be your ticket to getting published. Your fresh angle may be the industry you target or the way you handle the subject. Whatever you use as a twist, point it out in the query letter.

One way to conceive a new angle for a not-so-new subject is to invert the idea 180 degrees. Look through old journals and magazines to find articles on your subject. Then reverse their titles and see what you can do with them. For example, the subject and title of "The Power of Positive Thinking" can be rewritten as "The Consequences of Negative Thinking." "Overcoming Failure" can be changed to "How Failure Can Be Good for You."

Your angle does not have to be exotic or revolutionary. A common approach is the "new-and-improved" article that updates readers on developments in a field. Hot trends, new technologies, and recent research findings can give your article enough originality to make it marketable.

Writing query letters reduces your research time but does not eliminate it. The best way to impress an editor is to provide facts and statistics to support your concept. When researching an idea, investigate both the topic and your target market. Knowing who you are writing for will increase your chances of getting published.

Writing the Query An effective query must start strong and keep up the pace to the end. This does *not* mean it should read like advertising hype. On the contrary, your words have to be based in reality. A strong query letter gives the editor all the information quickly, accurately, and in a manner that piques his interest. Think like a journalist when you write. Cover the Who, What, Where, When, and How of it. Put your most important piece of information first.

The query should contain three main sections: the lead paragraph or hook, the summary, and the author's bio. In other words, tell the editor the story, why he should buy it, and why you are the person to write it.

The Hook A good lead paragraph should sell an editor on your idea and provide an example of your writing ability. If you can hook an editor with one paragraph, chances are good that you can write an article that will interest the publication's readers. The best way to open a lead paragraph is with startling statistics. This is not unlike giving a speech in which you begin by grabbing the audience with a compelling statement or question. Some leads quote a famous person, refer to a dramatic event, or tell a brief but relevant joke or anecdote. Jokes and anecdotes are risky. If you choose to use one, make it nothing less than great.

Whatever you choose for a lead, it has to captivate and set the style for the rest of the article. A lively, informal piece needs a lively, informal query. If it's going to be a straightforward how-to article, use a serious and businesslike query. Here is an example of a lead paragraph that packs a wallop:

> He may not be able to leap tall buildings with a single bound, but Tony Alessandra is considered a superman of the professional speaking world. In the last thirteen years, Tony has delivered more than 1,200 speeches. Between his speaking fees and product sales, Tony earns more than most CEOs, more than most doctors, and more than twice as much as the President of the United States. And people don't shoot at him; they give him standing ovations. How does he do it? Top-notch marketing and talent. Both can be learned. My proposed article, "Dr. Tony Alessandra, a Marketing Guru," will show your readers how to take their consulting and speaking businesses to new heights.

The Summary Paragraph Once you have captured the editor's attention, move directly to the description of the article. This section must convince the editor that you know your article's content and direction. Discuss the points to be covered, provide facts and figures if necessary, and include any quotations that will make your point stronger. A summary paragraph would sound like this:

> The proposed article will detail the proved marketing strategies developed over the last ten years by Dr. Tony Alessandra. It will cover the philosophy and execution of direct mail campaigns, prospecting, article publication and syndication, brochure design, program packaging, and fee structures. In addition, readers will be told in Tony's own words what they can to do to improve the content and delivery of their speeches and seminars.

Another format for the summary paragraph is the bullet formation. It describes the main idea and then lists the subjects to be covered, as in this query on the therapeutic effects of humor:

- **Humor as a Pain-Reliever.** The numbing effect laughter has on the body due to the secretion of natural pain killers called endorphins.

- **The Function of Humor in the Workplace.** The many uses of humor to improve cooperation and communication, decrease stress, and stimulate creativity.
- **The Many Faces of Humor.** Knowing when and how to draw the line between laughing with someone and laughing at someone.
- **How to Develop Your Sense of Humor.** Five concrete exercises the reader can practice to begin thinking funnier.

To round out my routine, I will provide relevant one-liners from interviews with Bob Heckle, a professional comedian, and Sam Gross, the owner of a local comedy club.

Heed these additional tips for your query:

- If you intend to interview people, name them, and give their credentials.
- Add any relevant sales points, such as your unique slant or the similarity of your article to others you have found.
- Be sure to mention the benefits of your proposed article to the readers.
- Ask your friends and colleagues what they would find valuable if you were to write this article. You may uncover some subtle selling points that didn't occur to you.
- Determine if there are significant dates or events to which your article might relate.
- Offer a working title. Avoid the temptation to spend sleepless nights trying to create the perfect title. Editors love to change them, so just provide a functional title that describes the article. The only bad title is, "The World's Greatest Article."
- Promise an industry exclusive.
- Provide the nuts-and-bolts information: the estimated number of words (based on 250 words per double-spaced page with one-inch margins), intended use of photos or illustrations, and when you can deliver the article.

The Bio After selling the article idea, sell yourself as the expert who should write it. Beginning writers quake in fear over the prospect of having to write a bio, their modest natures offended by the need to brag. This is not the time to be modest. Editors expect a bit of grandiosity in a bio. As long as it's realistic, blowing your own horn is acceptable.

The bio should be a convincing 100 words, give or take 20 percent. Start with publishing credits, if any. If you have none, don't worry; people aren't born with them. Instead, emphasize other qualifications: your professional experience, the type of work you do, your clients, and any other impressive details of your career, including awards. In a nutshell, explain why you are an expert in your field.

The qualifications for your bio can come from anything relevant—life experiences, jobs, hobbies, education, ethnic background, and even illness. Norman Cousins was an expert on the medical effects of laughter and positive emotions. His expertise stemmed from having used laughter and positive emotions to cure himself of a usually fatal disease. His book, *Anatomy of an Illness*, became a best-seller. Naturally, he did extensive research to flesh out his book, but the premise was based on his life experience.

Sending the Final Package

With only minor modifications, your query can be recycled through multiple submissions. Be sure, however, to customize each cover letter that accompanies your query. The cover letter will remind the editor of your telephone conversation. Keep the pleasantries to a minimum. Make a good impression with your article idea, not your social skills. Mention the query or article is enclosed, and you will contact him in a couple of weeks. If you think it is necessary, offer the editor an industry exclusive as an incentive to publish your article.

After two weeks, call the editor to ask if he received your materials and has had time to consider them. If his responses are positive, and he wants you to write an article, congratulations! Now discuss the details: your deadline, the length of the article, remuneration, and the length of the bio that will be at the end of the article. Be sure a bio will be allowed.

Unlike your query bio, your article bio should not only tell people who you are but how to reach you. For example, a bio for an article from this publication might add: "This article was adapted from *Publish and Flourish—A Consultant's Guide* by Garry Schaeffer and Dr. Tony Alessandra (John Wiley & Sons, 1992). For more information, call 1-619-584-1846."

Regardless of the outcome of your first attempt to sell an article, ask the editor if there are any special issues being planned. If so, find out when they will be published, their themes, and if you can submit article ideas for them. Being published in a special issue will provide you with a great deal of exposure. A query is a marketing tool. Like any other marketing tool, it must be executed with a high level of professionalism. Think of it as an audition in which you have two minutes or less to show your stuff. You have to be good.

The art of writing query letters can be learned. Short pieces such as queries are difficult to write in the beginning. The fewer words you are allowed, the better your writing skills must be to make a strong impression. Practice, get help, and stick with it.

SMALL STEPS TO SUCCESS

Work to Be Done   **Deadline**

1. Write a one-sentence positioning statement   _____
   for your article(s).

2. Locate the directories for professional jour-   _____
   nals and other publications to which you
   might submit an article.

3. Study the back issues of at least six publica- _____
   tions. Take notes on their content, style, and
   possible needs.

4. Contact editors by telephone or query letter.   _____

5. Write a one-sentence synopsis and hook for   _____
   a query letter.

6. Write a summary of your article idea.   _____

7. Write a 100-word bio of yourself.   _____

Get Started on This List Today

6

GETTING THE MOST MILEAGE FROM YOUR PIECE

Congratulations! Your article has been accepted, and it's time to put the deal in writing. You'll need to know something about periodical publishing contracts before you sign anything, and it won't hurt to know some of the ways a deal can be structured. Don't assume the contract that the magazine sends you is the last word. This chapter will show you what to ask for and how to extend the life of your article beyond its first publication.

TAKE AD SPACE INSTEAD OF MONEY

Payment is one of the more pleasant details to be discussed after your article is accepted. Some journals don't pay anything; others pay only a small fee. Compared to glossy national magazines such as *Reader's Digest*, *Playboy*, and *Cosmopolitan*, professional, trade, technical, and business journals pay peanuts. On the other hand, journals are easier to break into. Besides, you're not in it for the money. Your purpose is to build credibility and gain additional speaking engagements, consultations, or training work.

Your editor may welcome an alternative to paying you in cash. Offer to take advertising space in lieu of money. Try to talk your way into a half-page ad, with typesetting services included. You will come out far ahead in the long run. A half-page ad could bring you thousands of dollars of business and turn out to be better exposure than the article. The ad shown in Figure 6.1 has been successfully traded for articles.

If you can't get the ad space, insist on at least a decent-sized biography—sixty to one hundred words plus information on how you can be reached—at the end of the article.

After you iron out the details with the editor, the rest is easy. Write the article and submit it on time. If you are submitting a lot of queries or articles, devise a system such as a box of index file cards to keep track of them so you won't forget to follow up by telephone.

WHAT YOU ARE SELLING

Some journals and virtually all popular magazines buy "all rights," if you let them. This is an exclusive in the true sense of the word. The publisher has the right to do whatever he wants with your article, including selling it to another publication. You will be paid once, and that's it. After you sell all rights, you have no further ownership of the article. It becomes the property of the publishing company.

Total exclusives—that is, all rights—are usually given to publications that are prestigious enough to demand them. Their policy is to publish only articles that have not been previously published and will not be subsequently published. They believe their magazine or journal reaches the cream of the readership, so they don't think they should have to compromise.

Some journals and magazines that buy all rights will, after publication, release some rights if you submit a written request. They will evaluate their future need of the material and respond accordingly.

Selling all the rights to your article can be a good idea in two situations: You desperately want to be published, especially in a top-notch publication, or the article has such a narrow focus you doubt it would appeal to another publication. Regardless of your motive for giving away all rights, ideally you should receive a higher price

Make Your Relationships Work

Your Success depends on it...because people do business with people they like!

Dr. Tony Alessandra's *Relationship Strategies* is an effective system that **teaches you how to master behavioral flexibility—** the key to successful relationships.

- **Learn** how easy it is **to create chemistry and avoid conflict.**
- **Appreciate people more** by being able to see the world through their eyes.
- **Generate more business** with your greatest asset—your personality.

"When two people want to do business together, they don't let the details stand in the way."
—Phil Wexler & Tony Alessandra

PERSONAL SELLING POWER SPECIAL OFFER:

Relationship Strategies (Audio Cassettes): A fast-paced 12-lesson set that clearly explains how to recognize, respect and adapt to other people's behavioral styles.

How To Read People (Video): An entertaining 60-minute VHS tape of Dr. Tony Alessandra's highly acclaimed keynote speech. The perfect companion to the Relationship Strategies audio tape set.

Handy, laminated pocket guide that summarizes the behavioral styles. Refresh your memory with a glance.

ONLY $99.00!

Save $53.00 off the retail package price of $152.00!

P.S.P. BONUS

Mention Personal Selling Power and you will receive, **absolutely FREE:** *Relationship Strategies: How to Deal with the Differences in People.* This **100-page workbook** will help you gain a better understanding of yourself and sharpen your people skills.

UNCONDITIONAL 30-DAY MONEY-BACK GUARANTEE

To order* send $99.00 to:

Alessandra & Associates
P.O. Box 2767
La Jolla, CA 92038
(619) 459-4515

* For faster service and Credit Card Orders call TOLL FREE:
(800) 222-4383 (Outside Calif.)

Figure 6.1

for an exclusive. Realistically, however, in the beginning you will accept whatever payment is offered so you can get published.

An extra bonus to negotiate for, especially when offering an exclusive, is the front cover. Ask the editor if the cover is available. If it is, suggest a thought-provoking photograph that ties in with your article. Offer to provide a photograph or submit suggestions for the staff photographer to shoot. Remember, there may be ten articles in the issue but only one front cover. Think of all the publicity the cover would give you. Be courageous, and ask for it. The worst thing that could happen is you'd be laughed at. Big deal.

Selling all rights can be a bad idea because it prevents you from selling your article again. If you offer your best work to a second-tier publication in an exclusive deal, you may gain little and lose a lot. Be sure to balance the importance of getting published with the stature of the journal and your expectation of future sales of the article.

Sell First Rights and One-Time Rights Only

A better deal for the writer is to sell "first rights" and "one-time rights." First rights entitle the publisher to the exclusive first-time use of the piece. After it appears in the publication, you can do whatever you wish with the article. When you sell it again to another publication, you then would offer "one-time rights"—the right to publish it once. The objective is to sell it to as many publications as you can for years to come. You might also decide to rewrite it as a chapter in a book.

Industry Exclusives

An industry exclusive is a variation of the theme of selling first rights. Offering an industry exclusive is appropriate when you're trying to sell an article you've already written, not one you will customize for a specific journal.

By offering an industry exclusive, you are telling the editor he will have the first and only shot at publishing the piece in his industry. You promise to resell the article only to journals outside the field. In effect, you are dangling the carrot of exclusivity while holding onto your right to sell the article again to another market. This is the best of both worlds.

Offer industry exclusives only to publications that have enough prestige to deserve it. Don't give away exclusives as a bargaining chip to get your foot in the door unless you absolutely must. If you do, don't give away the rights to your best article; otherwise you could lose a powerful marketing tool.

When you give an industry exclusive, send two copies of a contract when submitting the article and be sure to get a signed copy back from the editor or publisher. Tony Alessandra uses the contract illustrated in Figure 6.2. (The names and titles in parentheses are fictitious examples.)

USING YOUR ARTICLE AS A MARKETING TOOL

You may have a beautiful, glossy, four-color brochure with professionally written copy, dazzling graphics, and a charismatic photograph, but nothing will sell you better than a book or an article. Having your name in print is an accomplishment everyone respects.

After your article appears in the professional journal of your dreams, use the reprints as promotional literature. You will increase your professional credibility and share the prestige that comes with being associated with that journal. The esteem bestowed on the journal will spill over onto you. From an advertising standpoint, the perception will not be that you have made any claims about yourself but that the journal has made them for you. The article will no longer be perceived as having been written by you; it will appear to be written about you.

Reprints are copies of the published article that are printed on glossy paper and have an appearance similar to the original journal pages. You can order reprints from the journal that published the article or have them printed yourself. Ordering from the journal will save a lot of time but may cost a little more. If the journal was produced in color, definitely have the journal produce your reprints. It would be an expensive waste to start over with a printer who would need new (and very costly) color separations and camera-ready layouts. Consider trading the article for 100 to 500 reprints. It doesn't hurt to ask.

If you want to reprint the article yourself, you must obtain written permission from the publisher or editor. Reprinting without permission is a violation of the journal's rights. Some publications

---

RELEASE & AGREEMENT

The undersigned author represents and warrants to (Smith Publishing Co.) that; he is the author of the enclosed article entitled ("Understanding the People Puzzle") proposed to be published in (*Genetic Engineering Monthly*): to the best of the author's knowledge, the article(s) submitted will not infringe on anyone else's copyright or other rights and will not contain any libelous material; he has the unqualified right to authorize publication of said article(s) for publication by (Smith Publishing Co.), its assignees and/or nominees. It is expressly agreed that any article or series of articles published in (*Genetic Engineering Monthly*) shall be considered the sole property of Alessandra & Associates, Inc., and the copyright shall remain the sole property of Alessandra & Associates, Inc. It is further agreed that (Smith Publishing Co.) may use the author's name and photograph in connection with any promotional activities. (Smith Publishing Co.) grants permission to said author to publish said article(s) outside of the (medical technology) industry, except for the publications mentioned below (to be filled in by editor):

(*Horizons in Science*)
(*The Laboratory Report*)

The aforementioned constitute the only publications where the use of the following (series of) article(s) would be prohibited:

("Understanding the People Puzzle")

Alessandra & Associates, Inc.

_____   _____
Name of Publication   Tony Alessandra, Ph.D.

_____   _____
Address   Date

_____
Signature of Ed./Publisher

_____
Date

Figure 6.2

will refuse to grant permission because they want you to buy reprints from them.

The advantage of having your own printer produce the reprint is that you can control the layout and design. Adding your logo to the first page and an expanded bio to the last page adds impact and makes it appear like a brochure.

When you want to impress a prospective client, send a brochure and a reprint (unless, of course, you have a book to send). The best type of selling allows the prospect to convince himself that you are the person to do business with. There is no sales message as powerful as the nonselling message contained in an article or book. Reprints offer proof of your credibility and expertise. It is impressive and flattering that your subject is important enough to the industry to merit publication.

Reprints can be used to impress book publishers and literary agents as well. When you send a book proposal to a publisher or agent, it looks good to be able to back up your bio with proof you have been published. If you have many published articles to your credit, don't send them all. List them on a separate sheet, and enclose the most impressive.

Reprints are excellent addendums to your brochure for trade shows and conventions. You will need plenty of them, so your initial order should be 500 to 1,000.

Reprints have a useful life of about two or three years. After that, they are too old to be impressive. People start to wonder why you haven't had anything published recently. You can rest on past laurels only for a finite amount of time.

SYNDICATION

Syndication in this context means selling one article to many journals after the initial publication. Imagine having a thousand reprints stacked up in your garage and the rights to resell the article. You now have a product to sell that will bring you additional income and exposure.

To capitalize on the work you have done already, write a cover letter and include a synopsis of the article. The letter does not have to be a query because the marketability of the article has already been demonstrated. Simply tell the editor why the article is appropriate for his journal. Naturally, you will have to research the journal and its market—not only for yourself but to convince the editor. In your letter, you can offer to revise the original article to custom tailor it for this particular publication's readers, but realize this will take more of your time. If you are busy, think twice before offering to revise an article, especially if no payment is offered.

The better your article is, the better your chances are of syndicating it. When you write your article, keep the following hints in mind and your piece will have a longer shelf life:

Give it broad appeal. An article that appeals to a large market will find its way into more publications than a highly specialized article. You have to strike a balance between two extremes: writing a narrowly focused article for a specific journal or writing one so general no one wants it. As an expert in your field, you should know what elements will make your article appropriate to many types of readers.

The easiest way to revise an article is to edit on a computer. The word processor allows you to search quickly for key words such as *manager* or *salesman* and replace them with others for another market. If you choose this route, read the article to make sure the substitutions make sense.

Write in a timeless style. A timeless subject, unlike a timely one, is not dependent on current events, the economy, or other trends to keep it alive. A timeless article is as relevant and marketable three years from now as it was the day it was written. If you deal in the type of subjects that are long-lived, write articles in a manner that will also be long-lived.

One way to avoid putting an out-of-date stamp on your article is to handle dated information carefully. If you are writing in 1987 and referring to 1986, don't write, "Last year, mutual funds outperformed the stock market by 32 percent." Instead, write, "In 1986, the stock market was outperformed by mutual funds." When discussing money and prices, give perspective by including the date. Instead of "This service will cost you $500 per month," say, "In 1986, this service cost $500 per month."

Use easily updated facts. If you sell a reprinted article years after if was written, you may have no choice but to update some of the statistics, prices, or other information. If the article was written with ease of update in mind, the revisions will be a snap. Easily updated information includes quotations from readily accessible experts, data from public sources and libraries, and statistics from newspapers and government publications. Quotations from inaccessible people and data from private organizations that no longer exist are the most difficult information to update.

BE ORGANIZED

Submitting one or more articles to journals and magazines takes a bit of organization if you want to maintain control of your work. There are two systems to set up in the beginning: a tickler file, such as an index card file, to remind you of follow-up telephone calls that have to be made and a simple chart to track your articles from submission to publication.

The chart system can be set up easily on a computer spreadsheet such as Lotus 1-2-3. Create a grid or spreadsheet. Label the top "Journals" or "Publications." On the left, vertically down the page, write "Articles." Each horizontal row will be a different article; vertical columns will be places you've sent it. In each box, write the dates the article was submitted, returned, or accepted and published. (See Figure 6.3.)

This chart can also be used in your market planning. Instead of filling in the publication's name after you have submitted an article, fill in the names of publications to which you plan to submit articles. Market planning will require more research; it will also motivate you to produce more articles, especially if you create deadlines for yourself and write them on the chart.

The keys to marketing are research and persistence. You have to target the proper journals, contact them relentlessly, and follow up until you sell an article. This process is mandatory. If you do not have the time to conduct the research and make the calls, hire someone to do it part time. Placing articles is as important as every other type of marketing and promotion you are undertaking.

PUBLICATIONS

	Professional Management Journal	Business Today	Sales & Service Monthly	Customer Service Journal	Management Assoc. Journal
A Ethics in the '90's	Query sent 1/14 Article sent 2/10 Accepted 2/30 Paid $200 4/1				Query sent 5/5
R Service: **T** Bottom-Line **I** Payoff			Article sent 9/5 Rejected 9/27	Query sent 2/22	
C Recruiting the **L** Sales Force			Query sent 10/10		
E Stress and **S** Productivity			Query sent 11/15		
Service Dilemmas and Solutions			Query sent 12/1 Article accepted 1/5	Query sent 11/14 Article sent 12/3 Paid $100 1/15	

Figure 6.3

SMALL STEPS TO SUCCESS

Work to Be Done   **Deadline**

1. Write a twenty-five-word bio that will appear   _____
   at the end of your article.

2. Create a full-page ad that would appear in a   _____
   professional journal in lieu of payment for
   your article.

3. Make a list of clients and prospects to whom   _____
   you would send a reprint of your article if it
   were published.

4. Go back to the directories of publications and   _____
   find prospects in other industries to whom
   you could submit articles.

Get Started on This List Today

7

RESEARCH MADE EASY

There are few other elements as important to writing a book as research. Most articles and books are built on solid research. After all, no one knows everything, except perhaps William F. Buckley, Jr. and Phil Donahue.

Research will make your work accurate and credible. Accuracy is indispensable in nonfiction writing. Never generalize without backing up your claims with statistics, quotations, examples, and other credible sources.

No expert relies solely on experiences for the content of articles and books. Like everyone else, you have to increase your credibility by providing facts that go beyond your experience. You must do your homework to support conclusions with data gathered from other sources, and there are many sources to tap.

MAGAZINES AND NEWSPAPERS

Of the many kinds of research, the most obvious type is library research. A less obvious but equally valuable form of research is the daily curiosity that motivates you to listen to the radio, watch television news, read the newspaper, and generally stay in touch with the world.

Newspapers and magazines are excellent sources of information. They are forever printing technical, medical, business, and human interest articles in addition to the news. Peruse as many magazines as possible, especially those related to your field. Cut out articles that will strengthen your own work. Expand your research capabilities by enlisting the help of friends and relatives to collect relevant articles for you.

LIBRARY RESEARCH

The idea of spending hours in the library researching an article or book chapter is a daunting thought to most people. But research does not have to be drudgery. There *are* ways to make it easier.

One way is to hire someone to do it for you. This is easy if you can afford it, though you may miss information that only you would recognize as relevant. If you hire someone, keep in mind the best researchers are experienced writers, good students, or librarians. Avoid helpers who hate library research, even if one is your spouse who will work for free.

The second, and better, way is to organize yourself and develop a curious attitude. Your curiosity will grow as you become more familiar and comfortable with the resources in the library. Organization is a learnable skill, so stay tuned.

STEPS TO EASY RESEARCH

Like any other skill that does not come naturally, organized research requires learning the basic steps that will make you efficient and effective. Some of these steps may seem elementary; others will be new to you. Heed them all, and you will cut your research time in half.

Determine the Purpose of the Research

It is important to pinpoint your audience for the research. Although you may use the same information sources for different projects, your intention will determine what kind of eyes you look through while you read.

When researching a broad topic, your internal sensor will be less selective as you read. You will frequently stop for digressions and explore a wide range of topics. If your research is highly focused, fewer words will be relevant to your scanning and selecting eye. You will skip over and ignore more material. For example, if you were researching a topic as broad as stress, you would be on the lookout for everything even remotely related. If you were interested only in the relationship of stress and backaches, your selectivity would increase.

To save time, know exactly what you are writing about before going to the library. Researching an article on stress in general will take much longer than finding information on the effects of stress on blood pressure.

Define Your Purpose

People write books and articles for many reasons, aside from the desire to make money or promote themselves professionally. Some of these reasons include teaching others how to do something, entertaining others, exposing a person or political event, theorizing and disseminating information, and persuading, motivating, or inspiring. An article can incorporate several purposes, but there is usually one primary reason. Isolating the overarching reason you are writing will help direct you to the appropriate sources in the library.

Control Your Research Time

Inexperienced researchers sink into a morass of information, most of it irrelevant. This is a time waster. The skills you learn in this section will help you avoid getting bogged down. Taking too much time, of course, is a relative concept. It is helpful to know what a "normal" amount of research time is. Otherwise, how would you know if these research tips were helpful?

Estimating the amount of research time necessary for a specific article or book chapter is difficult. People read, think, and write at different rates; different types of writing require different amounts of data; some people digress more than others. One writer we knew was prone to long digressions. In fact, he once went to look up a word in the dictionary and was never heard of again. Now *that's* a digression.

Individual differences aside, there are some generalizations that can be made. A minimum of three hours is usually required to become acquainted with a new subject. This includes finding the appropriate journal indexes, getting the articles, skimming the articles to determine their relevance, photocopying some articles, and maybe having time to read some of them fully in the library. Researching specific information or more familiar topics will take less time.

The length of the planned manuscript also affects research time. A general rule is one hour for every page, in addition to the initial three-hour get-acquainted time, if necessary. A four-page article on a new topic should take no more than seven hours (three hours get-acquainted time plus one hour for each of the four pages).

One way to reduce the amount of research time is to pare down the topic; consider writing less and giving it more impact. But never compromise the piece by substituting opinions and generalizations for hard facts and tested theories.

Outline Your Subject

An outline serves many purposes. As we saw in Chapter 4, it directs your thoughts while you write and gives you a sense of direction during the research phase by specifying the general areas in which you need facts, statistics, and quotations. If you are researching an unfamiliar topic, you may have to browse a while before developing a preliminary outline.

Turn Your Outline into Research Questions

From your outline, prepare a list of questions that need to be answered. Keep the questions at hand and continually refer to them during your research to help you home in on what you need.

When researching a subject on which you are already an expert, devise a list of questions that an audience typically would ask when you give a speech, training program, or consultation. Increase the number of questions and add information as you browse through periodicals.

Questions to guide your research should start generally and become more specific. A list of questions on the pain-relieving effect of laughter might look like this:

- Researchers involved in laughter research.
- Their findings on laughter and pain relief.
- Specific body chemicals involved.
- Physical benefits of laughter.
- Type of laughter stimulation used in studies.
- Implications for hospital patients.

Preparing a long list of questions may seem unecessary, but it will save you hours of library time. The list will prevent you from plowing through piles of journal articles and taking superfluous notes. Additionally, as you prepare the questions, you will develop a feeling for the relative importance of each. You will be able to prioritize questions and subjects and determine which do not need to be addressed at all. You will think of alternate sources of information and gain insight into your subject.

Determine the Type of Information Needed

After you have prepared a list of research questions, determine the types of answers needed for each question: scientific research findings, historical perspectives, names of famous people, facts, opinions, quotations, statistics, or anecdotes.

Determine how old your data can be. If you are looking for the most up-to-the-minute developments on a topic, don't use books. The information they contain is typically at least a year old. Magazine articles appear current but generally contain information at least six months old. When researching a timely subject such as business, the stock market, world affairs, or economics, find fresh and accurate alternative sources. Daily and weekly publications are excellent sources; experts are the most current. (Interviews will be covered subsequently in this chapter.)

If your subject has not changed appreciably in the past year or you are seeking a historical perspective, use easy sources such as the *Reader's Guide to Periodical Literature* and the card catalog for books. (Appendix A contains a comprehensive list of information sources.)

An article sometimes requires a combination of general theory, historical perspective, and current information. In a speech or article, citing the most current trends is obligatory. Not everyone does enough homework to be able to say something timely such as, "Just last week, the FDA quickly approved DDI and signaled that it is now ready to be an active partner with drug companies in bringing AIDS medications to the market." A sentence like this would work only in a consultation, training session, or speech a week after the news broke. In an article, you would have to specify the date by saying, "On July 22, 1991, the FDA . . ."

Determine the Best Source of Information

There are three sources of information: primary, secondary, and tertiary. A primary source is an expert's words, written or verbal. A secondary source is a magazine, newspaper, or journal article. Books, movies, and television shows, including news reports, are considered secondary sources. A tertiary source is anything beyond secondary. Someone telling you about a magazine article would be a tertiary source. Never use tertiary sources. If you can't find the time to obtain primary or secondary sources, delegate the research.

The most impressive way to research a book or article is to find primary sources. The closer to the source of knowledge you get, the more authority your work will have. Primary sources have several important advantages.

Reliability Pearls of wisdom gleaned directly from an interview with an expert are accurate and authentic. Quote your authority carefully and precisely. Paraphrase to relate the generalizations and background information.

Timeliness The data you obtain from the horse's mouth will be as fresh as hay in a barn, or maybe fresher. In some fields, such as biotechnology and computers, developments occur so quickly that last month's news may already be obsolete. This is not an exaggeration. Remember that there is often a six- to eight-month lag between the time the article was written and the publication date. The best way to find out the latest news is to make telephone calls and pursue the experts.

Specificity Secondary sources rarely speak directly to the research question you would like to answer. An interview allows you to ask specific questions about your subject.

When writing, avoid the temptation to use hearsay or common knowledge. It is amateurish to say, implicitly or explicitly, "Of course, everyone knows that . . ."

Use the Most Specific Sources First

As schoolchildren, we were taught to use encyclopedias and the *Reader's Guide* as information sources for research papers, but these are not the best sources for the specific, in-depth information required in an article or book written by an expert. Use these sources only if you want to read an overview or a popularization of a subject.

For serious information, identify professional journals. If you need historical information on someone, read the person's biography. To discover books written on a subject, consult a bibliography. There are bibliographies on everything under the sun. To find out if there is a bibliography on your subject, consult the *Bibliography of Bibliographies* or the *Bibliography Index*.

GETTING YOUR ACT TOGETHER

Most people go to the library and conduct their research in an unorganized fashion. Planning ahead and being organized before and during your research will decrease your time and stress.

Use a Research File

A file can consist of a box of index cards or a looseleaf notebook. The idea is to have the file system correspond to the research questions you've developed. Number the questions. As you uncover information, number a new section of the notebook, and put your notes there. If you are using index cards, start a new card for each question.

Keep a Running Bibliography

Most business and professional journals and magazines do not require the use of notes or a bibliography. Nevertheless, it is a wise practice to keep track of references as you use them. If you have to furnish a bibliography, a system will expedite the compilation. Your system will also be a personal reference system to help you find sources of information, quotations, and statistics.

Design your own reference sheet to provide space for all the information you could possibly want on each source, and make photocopies of it. For each publication, fill in a reference sheet and number it. Insert the number in your research file under the appropriate subject for future reference. The model shown here can be used.

```
┌──────────────────────────────────────────────────────────┐
│               MASTER REFERENCE SHEET                       │
│   Project _____   Reference #_____      │
│   Title _____   Author _____      │
│   Call #_____    Pages Used _____      │
│   Publisher _____   Date _____      │
│   Comments _____       │
│   _____         │
│   _____         │
│   _____         │
└──────────────────────────────────────────────────────────┘
```

Under "Comments," write the value of the source and your intentions for its use (e.g., quotations, statistics, or anecdotes). Note what topic or subtopic the source refers to. For quotations taken from a source, note the exact page number for future reference.

How to Use Reference Sheets

The advantages of a research system that includes reference sheets will unfold as you proceed with your work. To ensure you use the full potential of the sheets, follow these guidelines:

• When taking notes from a source, write down the reference number and author first; then take notes:

> #5, Smith, p.4, "Success is a state of mind that can be acquired." "The development of a positive attitude requires practice."

• When photocopying, immediately write the reference number at the top of the page.

- When making notes on file cards or in a notebook, use reference sheets as a time-saving device. In your notes, instead of entering an entire quotation or passage, write, "see source":

    #5, Smith p.4, Use long quote and explanation of success
    and mental attitude. See source.

- Interviews can be keyed to your notes. Give each interview a number, and treat it like any other source of information. In your notes you can enter:

    #5, Smith interview, p.3. See comment on success.

- When quickly writing the first draft of your article, save time by referring to a reference sheet. A first draft might look like this:

    It's easy to change your attitude. Dr. (first name?) Smith
    of *tk* Univ. says (#5, Smith, pg. 5 quote).

You can see how handy the reference sheet will be when it is time to fill in the information you forgot, such as the person's first name, university affiliation, and the exact quotation.

Photocopy Instead of Taking Notes

It takes a fraction of the time to photocopy an article than to read it and take thorough notes. Photocopy as many articles as necessary; then read and highlight them at home. If you read a photocopied article in the library, circle the relevant parts so you will not have to reread the entire article later. Use a time management technique: Bring material for research with you when you know there will be some waiting time that would otherwise be unproductive.

WHERE TO FIND WHAT YOU'RE LOOKING FOR

The best place to do research is in a university library—and the bigger the better. University libraries have indexes, directories, and journals for everything from Aardvarkology to Zzzzology (the study of sleep). Don't hesitate to ask the librarian for help. You'll be amazed how much more you will uncover when you let a librarian be your guide.

The number of journals in a major library is staggering. Some examples of indexes to professional journals are *Psychological Ab-*

stracts, Index Medicus, Education Index, and *Social Sciences and Humanities Index.*

Many libraries keep files of brochures, newspaper clippings, and miscellaneous loose pieces categorized by subject. The location of these vertical files is not as obvious as the indexes or card catalogs, so ask for them.

Using Computer Databases

Databases are large, computerized sources of information. Most university libraries can access them so you can search them for articles relevant to your topic. A few of the databases available are INFORM and Management Contents for business subjects, MEDLINE for medicine, and the National Institute for Mental Health (NIMH) for mental health. The New York City Public Library has a computer and database that is free to the public. It may well be worth the cost of a long-distance telephone call to use it.

To search a database, choose key words that you want the computer to search for. Then specify a database and a time period to be searched. For example, you might look for all the articles published between 1980 and 1985 that have the word *stress* in the title. The operator instructs the computer to find and list all articles that conform to your specifications.

At first, this may seem like a great convenience, and it is; however, there are two major problems. The first is that fees for hooking up to databases are high and accrue by the minute. If you think a taxicab ride in a traffic jam is nerve-racking, you had better take two Valium before watching a computer search. It can set you back $200 faster than a blackjack table can.

The second drawback is that the computer is not psychic. It does not have the ability to determine if an article is relevant. Consequently it will waste your money listing a lot of irrelevant references. You may end up with hundreds of article titles with the word *stress*, but only a fraction of them will be useful to you. There's no way around that.

The majority of the work takes place after the computer prints out a list of article titles. Someone has to spend hours finding and reading the articles to determine if they are relevant. There is one way to avoid this tedious and time-consuming phase. When you order the database search, have the operator instruct the computer to print out a summary (abstract) of each article along with its title. This will enable you to determine immediately if the article is worth pursuing. Printing out the abstract will take more time and cost more money. Depending on your finances, you may be better off searching trade publications yourself and leaving the computer searches to those who have six-figure grants to burn.

Identifying Special Interest Groups

Special interest groups have the latest and most comprehensive information on their cause and related industries. Write or call them to request information or interviews. To find groups in your field, consult the directories available in your library, such as the *Thomas Register of American Manufacturers*, *The Encyclopedia of Associations* (for trade and professional associations), and the *Foundation Directory* (for nonprofit organizations). If you plan to call instead of write, call the toll-free directory assistance (800-555-1212) to see if the organization has an 800 number.

When contacting an association to request information or an interview, keep the following guidelines in mind:

- Identify the person to contact, and call or write directly to this person for the best results.
- Explain your project, and describe how you will use the information you are seeking.
- Explain why you have chosen that particular group or person for your request.
- Pose specific questions. If you are requesting an interview, ask if the person would like to see the questions in advance.
- If you have a deadline, let the person know what it is.

Local corporations and universities are excellent sources of experts on many subjects. If you give enough notice and have a courteous, professional approach, most executives and professors will find the time to meet with you, especially if your article or book will give them some desired publicity.

HOW TO MAKE THE MOST OF INTERVIEWS

Conducting a comfortable, efficient interview requires some preparation on your part. The more you know about your interviewee and area of expertise, the smoother the interview will go. Your goal should be to get the most information in the least amount of time. Before the interview, define for yourself the reason you are interviewing this person. When you know what you are seeking, you will be able to give the interview a sense of direction.

The Personal Interview

Let the expert know what you are striving for. Showing all your cards before the interview will reduce its spontaneity but give the interviewee a chance to do any necessary homework. He may surprise you with useful statistics, a pithy story, or a visual aid.

Go into the interview with a list of questions, but use them as a guide, not as a script. Let the conversation ebb and flow. Encourage the expert to talk at length, but keep him from digressing too much. Ask for statistics, examples, names of other experts, and other relevant information. *Don't ask for information you can find on your own in the library.*

Complex questions are usually left partially unanswered, so keep questions simple and to the point; break them down into manageable increments. Avoid closed-ended questions—those that can be answered with a yes or no. Ask open-ended questions that require explanations.

To elicit good quotations, go over your questions in advance, and edit them to elicit specific and informative replies. Don't ask, "Is football a danger to boys in high school?" Ask, "How many football-related injuries did you have last year?" Don't ask, "Do you plan to stay in politics?" Ask, "How do you see your record as mayor affecting your race for the governor's seat?"

Do some homework about the expert and his field. If there is technical jargon, learn it. If the expert has been published, familiarize yourself with his ideas before the interview. Familiarity is the second best form of flattery.

Whether you should tape-record the interview or take notes is debatable and a matter of personal preference. Tape recorders have the following benefits:

- They don't break the flow of the interview as does note taking.
- You are free to listen carefully and respond rather than being distracted with writing.
- They don't miss a word and allow you to provide the interviewee with an exact transcript of the interview, which is something you should always offer.

There are disadvantages to tape recorders too:

- There is the possibility of mechanical problems. Recording an interview and later discovering a blank tape can be a major set-back.
- They make some people nervous, which may change the content and value of the interview.
- Transcribing the tape requires additional time or expense.

If you plan to conduct a lot of interviews, invest in a good tape recorder. (See Chapter 16 for a detailed discussion of tape recorders, dictation, and transcribing.)

To maximize your time, avoid small talk. Get to the interview as quickly as possible. Don't waste your interviewee's time.

Listen to the answers. If you don't understand something, ask for clarification immediately. As you listen, think of questions that relate to the operative words in the answers. Your questions should come from a logical train of thought, not necessarily your prepared questions. Go with the flow.

Avoid the temptation to show off your knowledge. Drawing analogies, giving examples, and other manifestations of your own brilliance are appropriate only if given within the context of questions. Don't try to make yourself equal to the expert.

If appropriate, end the interview with a question such as, "Is there anything I've overlooked that you can add?" Ask your expert if there is anyone else he thinks you should interview on this subject. Asking for referrals for interviews will give you an advantage when contacting the next person. You'll be able to say, "Professor Gene-splice suggested I call you to talk about . . ." Better yet, if you have created a rapport, ask your interviewee to call or drop a note to a couple of people, encouraging them to meet with you.

An excellent example of this domino principle of interviewing is the luck we had in researching another book of ours. Persistence, patience, and an interesting concept got us an interview with Steve Allen. Toward the end of the interview, Mr. Allen was kind enough to suggest two other people who might provide interesting interviews. He stopped everything in the middle of the interview, picked up the microphone of his dictating machine, and quickly composed a couple of brief letters to these people. One letter was to comedian David Brenner. The other was to a producer who spoke to one of the actors of the television series "Hill Street Blues." A week and a half later, with one follow-up call, David Brenner returned our telephone call to set up an appointment to interview him. Within days of that interview, Dennis Franz of "Hill Street Blues" called to set up an interview. The degree to which Steve Allen's recommendations smoothed the way was impressive.

Toward the end of your interview, be sensitive to your interviewee's body language. He may be telling you the interview is over; don't overstay your welcome. Heed the subtle cues you observe, and wrap up the session quickly and graciously. As you are leaving, ask if you can recontact him if you discover any loose ends that need to be tied up.

Telephone Interviews

The further into the academic or business stratosphere you venture, the less likely you are to be granted an interview. Let's face it; big shots don't have the time to meet with everyone who calls or writes. Top CEOs not only have their "yes men" but also layers of "no men" below them who run interference.

When you write or call the expert you would like to interview, give the option of a telephone interview. You may be granted ten minutes on the telephone, whereas a half-hour in person would be out of the question. A surprisingly large amount of information— and usable quotations—can be obtained in a ten-minute telephone interview. If the topic being discussed is interesting enough, you may be able to stretch the call to twenty minutes or more.

The principles of personal interviewing apply to telephone interviews as well. Make an appointment with the expert's secretary for a good time to call. Send the interview questions in advance.

During the interview, don't take notes; instead, buy a telephone microphone for your tape recorder. It is a common courtesy to tell the interviewee you are recording the conversation. After the interview, transcribe the tape while his words are still fresh in your mind. If the recording quality is poor, your memory will fill in the gaps.

RESEARCH THAT MAKES YOU THE EXPERT

Let's say, hypothetically, that you want to study a question no one else has answered in the business or science literature. You can become an authority on that area if you conduct your own research and answer the question adequately.

One way to collect data is to survey the people affected by the question. If you were interested in the relationship between getting published and an increase in one's consulting, speaking, or training business, you could prepare a questionnaire and send it to members of the National Speakers Association, the American Society for Training and Development, and the Institute of Management Consultants. You would collect a lot of interesting data and be able to draw some valuable conclusions. In one questionnaire, you could answer some of these questions:

- Have you ever published a book and/or articles?
- If you have been published, did you see a change in your business that can be attributed to your being published?
- How would you say your book or article affected your business? Increase? Decrease? No effect?
- If your business improved, what was the average yearly increase in the number of speaking engagements, consulting, or training jobs you conducted?
- What was the average increase in your yearly income after the publication of your article or book? What percentage was due to increased bookings? To book royalties?
- How did you write your book? Single authorship? Collaboration? Used a ghostwriter?

After you have compiled and analyzed the data, you will be—more or less—an expert on that issue. The more complex and significant the research, the more credibility you will gain. This is the premise for the publish-or-perish policy of most universities. It is not enough for a professor to be loved by students. Universities want their professors to be experts—preferably high-profile ones. The only way to achieve that is to conduct research and get published—no publications, no tenure.

Although research is time-consuming, in the long run you will save time. The savings will come later in the form of fewer rejections of your queries, articles, and books. A solid foundation will give you a stronger product that will appeal to editors and readers alike.

SMALL STEPS TO SUCCESS

Work to Be Done   **Deadline**

1. Subscribe to one or two more magazines or   _____
   professional journals.
2. Take a chapter or article outline and think of   _____
   research questions for it.
3. Set up a research file for a chapter.   _____
4. Design and photocopy master reference sheets.   _____
5. Go to the library and get a tour from the refer- _____
   ence librarian, or hire a research assistant.
6. Collect the research materials needed for your   _____
   first article.
7. Find one expert; contact and set up an ap-   _____
   pointment for an interview.
8. Identify the objectives of the interview.   _____
9. Develop interview questions based on objec-   _____
   tives.

Get Started on This List Today

PART THREE

Move On To Your Book

8

GETTING STARTED ON YOUR BOOK

Now that you've gotten your feet wet with articles, it's time to start thinking about writing a book. This is done the same way you accomplish any other goal, as we stated in Chapter 1:

> **The key to writing a book successfully is to break it down into small, manageable increments.**

A book isn't written in one fell swoop. The first step is to break it down into nonthreatening, manageable tasks. The next is to get started immediately. If a busy schedule prevents you from starting the project, either delegate some tasks (such as research), or commit yourself in writing to a starting date in the near future.

Merely intending to start your book is not enough; you have to identify a specific task and a time when you will do it. Nearly everyone says they would like to write a book someday. The difference between those who say someday and those who actually do it lies in accomplishing small steps, one at a time. Avoid setting a vague goal such as, "I will write my book by the end of the year." It won't happen. What you see as your mission is too large. You'll procrastinate indefinitely. Instead, say to yourself, "Tomorrow on the plane to Chicago, I'm going to brainstorm the contents of the book. Then I'm going to read the five articles that my secretary found in the library."

WHERE DO YOU START?

There are many steps in writing a book. An overview of eighteen steps will show you how easy it is to see the project in terms of many small pieces rather than as an overwhelming, amorphous project. The following list of steps is not meant to be comprehensive. Many more tasks will arise as you progress, but like any other project, simply add them to your list and get them done.

The Building Blocks of Book Writing

1. Define and focus your subject.
2. Target a market.
3. Create a working title and subtitle.
4. Brainstorm at least ten major ideas to cover.
5. Create chapter files for each major idea.
6. Check *Books in Print* for competition and the originality of your title.
7. Check bookstores and the library for similar books, and compile a list.
8. Brainstorm and outline each chapter.
9. Make a list of research needs for each chapter.
10. Get relevant books and articles at the library.
11. Write a book proposal and sample chapters.
12. Submit a proposal and sample chapters to a literary agent or publisher.

13. Write first drafts of other chapters.

14. Edit and rewrite first drafts.

15. Complete the first draft, and give it to friends and associates for feedback.

16. Revise the first draft, and submit it to some reviewers from your target market.

17. Revise the second draft based on reviewers' comments, and submit a final manuscript to an agent or publisher.

18. Visualize a best-seller and how it will boost your career and change your life.

Some of these steps depend on your overall plan for the book. For example, writing a book proposal and sample chapters will be unnecessary if you are going to self-publish or submit a complete manuscript to a publisher or literary agent. If you want to get a publisher's contract before you begin, do only the research necessary to write a proposal and a sample chapter. Then submit them to a publisher and wait. (See Chapter 12 for more information on this option, which we recommend.)

Do you really want to finish the book? If so, take your "to do" list one step further by establishing deadlines for each step. Define each goal so it is clear-cut and easily attainable. It is important to experience a sense of progress and accomplishment by completing steps that bring you increasingly closer to a finished book. Adjust the demands on yourself according to your schedule. If you can handle a lot of work, do it. If you feel overpressured by the deadlines, adjust them so you won't feel stressed rather than motivated. Don't try to overstep your capabilities. The last thing you want is for this project to become a source of frustration and anger.

STARTING FROM SCRATCH

As a consultant, speaker, or trainer, you build your programs the way writers write books—piecing together many ideas to form a whole. The concepts you discuss in consulting or training sessions come from your knowledge and experience, as well as ideas other people have disseminated. Writing a book requires you to find ways to put on paper all those things you say in your business. It's easier than you think.

Chapter Files

One of the first steps after outlining the major topics of your book is to create a file for each chapter. Use a file cabinet, manila envelopes, or something else so you have a place to store the materials and notes that will accumulate. Constantly work at filling up those files with good, current information.

Take Notes, Notes, and More Notes

Record every thought you have on your subject. As you immerse yourself in each concept, you will think of innumerable new and used tidbits of information that must be saved. As ideas arise, write them down, and put them in the appropriate chapter file. It doesn't matter if you use fancy twenty-pound bond paper or cocktail napkins for your notes as long as they are captured in some permanent and retrievable form.

Tape recorders are excellent tools for quickly capturing your thoughts. They are even better for dictating the contents of articles and chapters than for recording brief notes. But dictating entails twice as much work because someone has to transcribe the tapes. For this reason, tape recorders should be used primarily in situations in which speed is essential.

A collection of copious notes will vastly improve the quality of your manuscript. Leave no thought unrecorded. The form and substance of your book will be far superior to one written only with the ideas that come to you when you are sitting at the computer.

Writing the First Draft

Although we suggest you write a proposal before you begin writing the book as a whole, this is as good a time as any to discuss the issues concerned with beginning your first draft. Even when submitting a proposal, you'll need to include at least one completed chapter. In a sense, your book will already be underway even before you have negotiated a pre-project contract. In fact, there is no hard and fast line between writing your proposal and writing your book, and you may get a lot of prelimary draft work done for the book while writing your proposal.

The most difficult part of writing is sitting down and starting.

The question of where to begin always arises. Your research materials are organized, your outline is thorough, and theoretically you are ready to go. In reality, many writers get bogged down when facing an empty page.

You expect it to be easy to capture on paper what is in your mind, but it's not. When the right thoughts aren't forthcoming, you panic or freeze. Realize and accept from the beginning that the right words don't always come quickly, and they are usually not the first ones put on paper. That's why God created rewriting and editing. So accept the fact that perfection is never achieved immediately and effortlessly.

Another misconception many writers have is they will sit down and write what they already know. The truth is, writers sometimes write to know. *Writing is a process of exploration and discovery.* Edward Albee summed it up when he said, "I write to find out what I'm thinking." Part of the creative process in writing is discovering what unfolds as you write.

Writing Requires a Warm-up Period

The fact that good writing does not happen right away is a valuable insight. Writing is like playing a sport. Let's say that your sport is high jumping, and on a good day you can jump six feet. During a practice session, you know better than to start with the pole at six feet. You start at five feet and warm up to your goal of six feet.

Approach writing in a similar way. It is unrealistic to expect to sit down and immediately write a continual stream of well-organized ideas. Expect to start slowly. If you eliminate all interruptions, your momentum will increase until you are flying along happily.

Write Yourself a Letter

There are many ways to warm up your brain. Try writing a letter to yourself in which you describe the specific chapter on which you are working. Start out with small talk. Ask yourself how you've been, what's new, how your spouse and kids are. Then get to the meat. Tell yourself something about this chapter. Pose some questions, answer them, and keep going. This process will open the gates to a flood of productive writing.

Write Nonjudgmentally

The best way by far to get your literary wheels turning is to write as quickly as possible, making no judgments about what you've written. Your mind works much faster than your hands. The challenge is to get as much on paper as possible and as quickly as possible. Don't stop to search for the perfect word or to correct spelling errors; that can be done later. Now is the time for stream-of-consciousness writing. Follow your outline when you can, but remember you can always cut and paste later. You will be amazed by the speed and productivity that comes from this method of writing. The velocity of your writing will force unexpected thought associations to occur. This is creativity at work, and it is an exhilarating experience.

While you are speeding along, writing nonjudgmentally, you'll miss details that you will have to come back to fill in later. Perhaps you forgot how many feet are in a mile or the length of a light-year. To mark the spot, insert the symbol *tk*, which denotes "in the space provided." For example, "If a person's foot is a size 10 and there are *tk* feet in a mile, how many steps would it take to walk a mile?" The missing data can be researched and filled in another time. In fact, one day, if you find yourself lacking the motivation to sit and write, you can do the research necessary to fill in the *tk*'s.

Chew Bite-Sized Pieces

When you begin writing the first draft, follow an extensive outline that breaks the chapter down into small, manageable increments called subsections. If it makes writing easier for you, divide each subsection into increments so small that each one represents a paragraph. This would be an extremely detailed outline but would show you precisely where you are going with your ideas. This is an unusual way to write, but it helps some people organize their thoughts.

SMALL STEPS TO SUCCESS

Goals for Your Book
Work to Be Done   **Deadline**

1. Finish reading this book.   _____
2. Define and focus your subject.   _____
3. Think of a working title for your book.   _____
4. Go to the bookstore and library to research   _____
   the market and evaluate the competition.
5. Brainstorm at least ten major ideas to be cov-   _____
   ered in the book.
6. Create chapter files for each major idea.   _____
7. Brainstorm (cluster) chapter outlines.   _____
8. Obtain relevant books and articles from the   _____
   library.
9. Write the first draft of a chapter.   _____

Get Started on This List Today

9

ARE TWO HEADS BETTER THAN ONE?

Writing is not only an art; it is a business. If you self-publish, you are going to create a product that needs to be developed, manufactured, promoted, inventoried, priced, and sold. Each phase takes time and money, and there are legal implications that must be addressed every step of the way.

Although writing is, by nature, a solitary endeavor, you may have the opportunity to build a winning team that will take some of the loneliness out of it. Co-authors, literary agents, research assistants, editors, graphic artists, and printers are a few of the many people with whom you will deal as you take your book from concept to completion.

Collaborations, like marriages, work well for some people and are disastrous for others. On the pessimistic side, there are people who, like Agatha Christie, believe "where two people are writing the same book, each believes he gets all the worries and only half the royalties." Of collaborations, Evelyn Waugh said, "To me that's like three people getting together to have a baby."

Certainly there are productive, well-adjusted writing teams

who defy the laws of egocentricity or greed. In many situations, collaboration is either necessary or desirable: You are too busy to write a book and need the help of a co-author or ghostwriter; you are part of a team of experts who develops a book idea and shares the research and writing responsibilities equally; you may have written the first draft of a book and need a co-author to rewrite and improve it; you have written a workbook that can be expanded and turned into a book with the help of a ghostwriter. Innumerable circumstances prevail that dictate the use of collaborators. Keep an open mind and consider collaborations as a viable alternative to going it alone.

One advantage of a collaboration is the built-in diversity. You and your partner have different life experiences to draw upon. Each of you has strengths and weaknesses that should complement the other's. For example, you may be a conceptualizer, while your partner is practically minded and executes the ideas. Your writing styles may complement each other as well. You have a flair for metaphors and analogies, while your partner thinks in terms of facts and figures.

While diversity is an asset, partners also need to learn how to compromise. During the writing stage, you will be reading, editing, and possibly rewriting each other's work. There will be time when you will discuss changes and need to compromise. Rather than becoming defensive when your work is questioned, try to see the other person's point of view. This is a good exercise in objectivity and ego control. Ideally, both of you will become better writers from your partner's feedback.

There are other advantages to working with a partner. You can tackle more ideas in less time. Your co-author can act as a cheerleader, motivating you to start projects and stop procrastinating. The two of you will be able to brainstorm new ideas and expand your product lines.

If, even after reading this book, you still cannot muster the time, motivation, will-power, or organizational ability to write your own articles or book, you would be wiser to give away 50 percent of a finished product than to procrastinate forever doing it yourself.

HOW TO FIND A COLLABORATOR

Finding a collaborator is like finding a spouse. Some people effortlessly fall into a strong, long-lasting marriage; others search all their lives for their perfect match. There is no formula for finding a compatible writing partner. Word of mouth, trial and error, and the use of your best judgment are the best ways. Choose your partner carefully. A collaboration, despite its good intentions, can turn into an emotionally tumultuous relationship. If it produces a book, however, it is easier to justify the suffering than if the project dies.

Books, unlike children, do not develop indelible scars from the battles of their creators. If your partnership develops growing pains, stick with it, iron out the problems if you can, and produce that book. There is always something to be learned from a collaboration. If nothing else, you may decide you don't like to collaborate, although that is unlikely. You just need to find the right partner.

As a businessperson you are well connected to a network of professionals. Look within your network for someone who would like to collaborate on articles and books. If no one comes to mind immediately, ask around. Excellent candidates are people you met at conventions, business meetings, and trade shows.

USE A PROFESSIONAL WRITER

A professional writer may be your best choice for a collaborator. There are two ways to work with a professional writer. One way is to hire a ghostwriter, pay for the service, and take all the credit yourself. Ghostwriters' fees vary, so shop around. Some ask for a flat fee; others ask for a flat fee plus a percentage of the royalties. Everything is negotiable, but keep in mind that a ghostwriter makes or breaks the marketability of the book. There are lots of bad and mediocre writers. A great writer is more difficult to find and worth the extra money when you find one.

Another way to work with a professional writer is to ask him to write on spec. If your project holds a lot of promise, he may speculate and work for free in exchange for a healthy share of the royalties and his name on the book. The obvious advantage to this arrangement is you pay nothing up front. The disadvantage is that you have to share the glory and the income from the book.

There is no cut-and-dried way to decide which working relationship is better for you. Some of the variables to consider when making your decision are:

- Your book's potential.
- Its function in your career.
- Your publishing history, if any.
- The experience and talent of the writer.
- Your ability to pay a writer in advance.
- The speed with which you want a book written.

If you are writing your first book, the finished product will do more for your career if you are the sole author or at least the first author. If you can afford it, pay a ghostwriter so your name will be the only one on the book. The more names there are on the cover, the more diluted will be the credibility of each.

WHAT IS YOUR PARTNER'S TRACK RECORD?

When collaborating with a co-author, align yourself with the best possible ally. Choosing a writing partner is similar to choosing a tennis partner; you learn more when you hit with a better player.

Take into consideration your collaborator's writing ability and experience (both published and unpublished), expertise in the field, consulting, training, or speaking experience, exposure, time constraints, and genuine enthusiasm for your project. Weigh all of these factors and be open-minded. The best person for you may not be the most experienced. You may find someone who is inexperienced but talented and willing to work hard for relatively little money. On the other hand, a writer who has publishing connections and a lot of experience can offer insights that even the most earnest neophyte cannot. You have to evaluate your strengths and weaknesses concerning the writing and publishing process and find someone who complements you.

DETERMINE EVERYTHING IN ADVANCE, IN WRITING

Once you have chosen a writing partner, hash out the details. Don't assume anything, even if your partner is your best friend. Decide in advance who will do what, and set deadlines for every phase of the project. Some of the responsibilities to parcel out are:

- Research
- Interviews
- Transcribing tapes
- Conceptualization and outlining
- Writing first drafts
- Editing and rewriting
- Acquiring a literary agent
- Submitting the book to a publisher
- Negotiating the book contract

You and your collaborator also need to discuss the authorship, rights, and money aspects of the project. Some of the details to be ironed out include:

- The order of authorship
- Who will hold the various rights to the book
- What the advance and royalty split will be
- Who will appear to promote the book
- Who has the right to use the contents of the book for articles or speeches

After you have hashed out the legal details, put everything in writing. There are standard ghostwriting and collaboration agreements (see Appendix B) available in law libraries. Pages 98 and 348 of the first volume of *Lindey on Entertainment, Publishing and the Arts* are useful. These legal contracts can be used verbatim or modified to suit your needs.

THE IMPLICATIONS OF AUTHORSHIP CREDIT

The order of authors' names on the book cover can be a tremendous point of contention between partners. Everyone wants his name first. How do you decide who gets top billing? The nature of your working relationship and the individual contributions to the project will help determine the order of the names.

If you and your partner(s) are equals in knowledge and contribution, each of you deserves equal authorship. There are several possibilities on how to decide the order of your names, including alphabetical order, flipping a coin, or arm wrestling. If the genesis of the idea or the majority of the expertise lies with one of you, however, he deserves to be the first author. The other(s) can fight for subsequent position.

The way two or more names appear on the cover implies different roles to the authors. If both people are experts on the subject and equal contributors to the book, their names would appear as, "by Susan Scribe and Harry Hacker." Some people may infer the order of the names has some significance. The typical assumption is the first author is either more of an expert or the person whose idea started the book. Hence, the struggle to be first author.

If Susan Scribe were the only expert and wanted to make that clear while still giving Harry Hacker credit, she would use the form, "by Susan Scribe with Harry Hacker." *With* basically means, "as told to," and is commonly used on autobiographies. *With* implies Susan is the expert and Harry is the writer who made her knowledge readable. Before finalizing the negotiations on this issue, consider the implications carefully.

WORKING WITH YOUR PARTNER

It is essential that you trust your partner to work as hard as you will on his part of the project. Doubts and a lack of trust in a collaboration are like dry rot on a boat; they weaken its structure and make it unsafe. Communicate with your partner. If your load becomes too great, discuss the situation and redistribute the work rather than harboring grudges.

Realize the Risk of Collaboration

Collaborating on a book can put severe strain on a relationship. It could ruin a friendship or significantly weaken the bond between business partners. In the beginning, it is easy to think you will be able to dissociate your business and personal lives. It rarely happens; save yourself some grief.

Experiment with Writing Strategies

The way your collaboration functions will depend on your schedules, the nature of your agreement, the type of work being done, your proximity to each other, and your individual writing habits. When possible, experiment with different work habits to find the one that is most productive for both of you.

One modus operandi for team writing is for the two of you to work on the outline together and then divide the chapters so each of you writes half of the first draft. After the first draft has been written, swap your sections for critiquing and editing.

Another strategy is to write together. Develop a thorough outline; then while one of you writes, the other stands over his shoulder and makes suggestions. You can switch halfway through if that will give you a new perspective. If both of you prefer to dictate, have a dictating session. Turn on a tape recorder, and start talking about the book in as logical an order as possible. Later you can have the tape transcribed and rewrite what you have created.

Decide Who Will Deal with Editors

Editors are more comfortable dealing with one author rather than two or three members of a team. Decide who will be the business end of the team. When the time comes, that person will have to take copious notes of meetings and telephone calls with editors and share the information with the partner(s).

Decide How to Split Expenses

Writing a book is not always cheap; it often requires more than a computer and printer. There are interviews, research, travel, gas, photocopies, supplies, books, and other expenses. If two of you are hiring a ghostwriter, that expense will have to be divided as well.

When one of you makes more money than the other, he could offer to incur the expenses up front. In your collaboration agreement, include a clause to guarantee that person will be reimbursed from the publisher's advance. Another arrangement is to split all the expenses equally as they accrue.

Decide Who Will Prepare the Final Draft

There is more to submitting a manuscript than printing out and photocopying it. Someone has to proofread it. Someone has to create an index. Someone has to organize the camera-ready art, tables, drawings, and other graphics. There is a great deal to be done. To be fair, these tasks should be divided equally, but the arrangement is up to you. Or you could hire someone to take care of these details.

Keep Your Enthusiasm Up

Some writing teams split up the work, return to their homes, and don't see each other for six months, either for logistical reasons or out of choice. The healthiest team is one in which the partners continually refuel themselves with contact. While writing this book, we met an average of once a week to discuss concepts, marketing possibilities, and other details of the project. Afterward we always felt a renewed enthusiasm for the project.

Collaborations can be healthy, stimulating experiences. A productive, successful partnership will renew the faith in even the most jaded, reclusive writer. For a busy businessperson who aspires to writing a book, a collaboration is a way to do half the work to achieve your goal. An ongoing writing team can accomplish two or three times as many goals as one person. If one book makes you an expert, imagine what two books, journal articles, and audio and video products would make you—a star!

SMALL STEPS TO SUCCESS

Work to Be Done   **Deadline**

1. Evaluate your need for a collaborator.   _____
2. Write out your strengths as a writing partner.   _____
3. List the characteristics that are most important   _____
   to you in a collaborator.
4. List how you could find a collaborator.   _____
5. Inquire about a collaborator at your next asso-   _____
   ciation meeting, or put an ad in the newspaper.
6. Read Appendix B, "Sample Collaboration   _____
   Agreement."

Get Started on This List Today

10

SELL THE SIZZLE BEFORE THE STEAK

The ideal way to write a book is to be paid for it ahead of time. Based on your submission of a proposal, you may be able to negotiate a publisher's contract in advance. To make this happen, your idea has to be fresh and your proposal well-written. It is not unusual for publishers to offer contracts based on a proposal and sample chapter, especially to writers with track records.

An effective book proposal serves one purpose: It sells your book idea and your writing ability to the decision makers of a publishing house. The proposal does this in a succinct, informative style, with no sales hype. The content and professional preparation of the proposal sell the book, not the author's assurances that the idea is potentially a best-seller.

Your proposal must be written with *style*—in fact, the same style as the proposed book. If you are trying to sell a humorous book, you had better be able to make others laugh with the proposal. Otherwise, how will they know you have a great sense of humor?

There are basic ingredients that go into every book proposal.

The order in which these ingredients appear will depend on the assets of your proposal. If you are a published writer or otherwise well known, the strength of your book may come from who you are. In this case, you would sell yourself first and the book idea second. If the opposite is true—that is, the book idea is unique and marketable but your bio is not awe inspiring—sell the book concept first and yourself second.

The cover page of the proposal lists the title and author. In the lower-right corner, the author's address and telephone number or agent's telephone number are typed. Page one of the proposal contains the working title, alternate titles, a subtitle, the keynote (synopsis), and the beginning of either the bio or the theme section.

THE TITLE

The title is important as a sales tool because it immediately shows the editor how creative you are. The ideal title cleverly describes the book and catches readers' attention. Some subjects lend themselves to catchy titles; others need straightforward, descriptive titles. Do the best you can without getting corny or using clichés. Clever puns are acceptable.

If you have alternate titles in mind, list two or three beneath the working title. If you do not have alternate titles, don't make them up so you will appear prepared. If a publisher likes your book idea but does not like your title, the editor will suggest others.

SUBTITLE

Subtitles add information that the title cannot provide. A good subtitle positions the book and succinctly tells the reader what it is about. For instance, the subtitle of this book follows with selling information: "How to Boost Visibility and Earnings Through a Publishing Strategy."

THE KEYNOTE

The keynote is a one-sentence synopsis of the book. You should be able to describe your project in one sentence. (That way, you will sound smooth when people ask about it at cocktail parties and on radio and television talk shows.)

AUTHOR'S BIOGRAPHY

Depending on your experience, your bio for a book proposal will run from one-half to two pages. The best credentials are previously published books and articles. Everyone starts out inexperienced, however, so don't worry if you have no credits yet. Emphasize other qualifications, such as your reputation in your profession. For a detailed discussion of how to write a bio, refer to the appropriate section in Chapter 4. A good example of a proposal-type bio follows:

Garry Schaeffer is a freelance writer based in San Diego, California. His work has appeared in *Skin Diver, Trailer Boats, Seacoast, San Diego Magazine*, and *Reader's Digest*. Garry has collaborated on many books on sales and customer service. His creativity and light, conversational writing style have earned him a solid reputation as a sales communications consultant.

Dr. Tony Alessandra is one of the top sales and communications keynote speakers in the United States. In the last ten years, he has averaged more than 100 speeches each year and has received the prestigious C.P.A.E. award for speaking excellence from the National Speakers Association. Tony has co-authored more then 100 articles and several books, including *Non-Manipulative Selling* (Prentice-Hall, 1975), *The Art of Managing People* (Prentice Hall, 1980), and *The Business of Selling* (Reston, 1984). *Non-Manipulative Selling* has sold more than 105,000 copies and was revised in 1987 for publication by Simon & Schuster.

Tony has developed and performed in more than 50 audio and video programs and training films for such companies as McGraw-Hill, Walt Disney, Nightingale-Conant, the University of Southern California, and Simon & Schuster.

THE THEME

The theme is a one- to four-page description of the background, contents, and purpose of the book. This summary often includes the book's market analysis, although some authors prefer to discuss it separately. The theme should distill the essence of the book and serve as the primary sales presentation. It is in this section that the weight of the proposal lies. The theme is similar to a short, persuasive speech or essay.

Start with impressive statistics or a general statement. Focus on the book idea and explain why it is important and marketable. Be positive and enthusiastic without resorting to hype and hyperbole. An example of a theme follows:

After several years in business, many consultants, professional speakers, and trainers find themselves in the doldrums. They are established and doing what they want but not to the extent they would like. The question arises, *How do I make the leap to the position of having nearly all the business I want?* The answer is simple: Write a book.

Our book will teach readers how to write books and articles. It will take them through all the steps, from conceptualization and organization to research, writing, editing, and marketing. In addition, it will seriously address the psychological aspects of writing and teach readers how to play and win the mental game.

Consultants, speakers, and trainers were not born knowing how to deliver a keynote speech or conduct a training seminar. Writers are not born knowing how to write clearly or eloquently. Everyone—even the masters—starts from a state of ignorance. Those in the target market have an advantage; most have achieved the formidable goal of learning to give a presentation. There is no reason they cannot learn to write anything, from a short article to a lengthy book. *Publish and Flourish* will give readers all the ingredients they need to succeed and push their careers to the next level.

MARKET ANALYSIS

Some authors prefer to call this section a "Rationale." Whatever term is used, it explains why your book is necessary, where it will find its niche, and how it compares to books on the market. Competing books are mentioned by name, along with an explanation of the ways in which your book will be different and better.

If there are many competing books on the market, familiarize yourself with all of them, but in your proposal, discuss only the most similar ones. The example we have been using in this chapter—the book you're reading—had no competition. Following is our market analysis:

Publish And Flourish: A Consultant's Guide is targeted to consultants, professional speakers, and trainers who can be reached effectively through direct mail and bookstore sales. Preliminary research in the *Encyclopedia of Associations* has uncovered over 40 professional associations with almost 340,000 members who qualify as prospective buyers of this book.

The competition for *Publish and Flourish* is limited. While there are many "how-to-write" books on the market, *none* speaks directly to the markets we have targeted. Furthermore, most books are focused solely on *one* aspect of writing. *Publish and Flourish* covers every aspect of publishing that aspiring business writers need to know to get published.

The authors have amassed testimonials for *Publish and Flourish* from some highly noted experts:

Ken Blanchard, co-author of *The One-Minute Manager*

Nido Quebin, Professional speaker

Howard L. Shenson, a top management consultant

Terry McCann, executive director, Toastmasters International

Karl Albrecht, co-author of *Service America*

In addition, Tony Alessandra's reputation in the professional speaking world will give the book instant credibility.

The best thing you can do for your project is to create a strong angle that will position the book well for your publisher. You should be able to demonstrate a good understanding of the competition in your market segment. All writers must be in touch with their markets, regardless of their genre. Writing in a vacuum may work for poets and essayists, but fiction and nonfiction writers cannot take the chance of duplicating a book that has already been written.

ORGANIZATION

The next section of your proposal explains the nuts and bolts of the book. Under the heading "Organization," briefly tell the editor how many sections, chapters, and pages you anticipate. To determine the length your book should be, see what other writers have done with similar books. How long are they? What is appropriate for the subject and type of people who will read it? Make your book similar in length unless you have a good reason to be different.

The organization section also includes a chapter-by-chapter description of the book, including proposed chapter titles. No heading is required to introduce the chapters; they follow the nuts and bolts. Instead of showing you the entire organization section of the example proposal, a handful of chapters will suffice.

ORGANIZATION

Five Sections, 18 chapters, 70,000 words, innumerable insights.

Introduction

Fear as an obstacle to book and article writing is discussed briefly.

PART I: OF COURSE YOU CAN DO IT

Chapter 1: WHY YOU *MUST* GET PUBLISHED
       To promote your expertise.

Readers are shown how articles and books can increase their exposure, fill their calendars, boost their credibility, and increase their fees and passive income.

Chapter 2: WRITING IS A MENTAL GAME
How to edit your attitude to delete writer's block.

Procrastination, writer's block, motivation, visualization, affirmations, values, and other mental aspects of being a writer are discussed.

PART II: START WITH ARTICLES

Chapter 4: THE EASY WAY TO WRITE ARTICLES
Break them down into small increments.

Among other things, this chapter covers the nuts and bolts of articles. Also covered are types of articles, outlining, quotations, and various types of information.

Chapter 5: HOW TO POSITION AND MARKET YOUR ARTICLES
Use the techniques of effective product marketing.

Readers are introduced to the concept of positioning and shown how to target their markets and write query letters.

PART III: MOVE ON TO YOUR BOOK

Chapter 8: GETTING STARTED
First get organized, then outline and write.

This chapter addresses one of the most crippling obstacles for beginning writers, the question: Where do I start? Readers see how a book project is broken down into manageable steps, which serve as a blueprint for action. Writers are told how to overcome inertia to get their creative juices flowing.

Chapter 10: SELL THE SIZZLE BEFORE THE STEAK
Sell 'em, then write 'em.

As with articles, readers are encouraged to use proposals to sell their book ideas before they write the entire book. The contents and requirements of book proposals are discussed with examples from this book's proposal.

Chapter 13: BOOK CONTRACTS: CAVEAT SCRIPTOR!
We've translated legalese into everyday peoplese.

This chapter tells readers what to expect in a publisher's contract and explains the most common clauses.

PART IV: DEVELOP THE SKILLS OF A SUCCESSFUL WRITER

Chapter 14: STYLE: ADDING PANACHE TO YOUR POINT
Make your work powerful, credible, and readable.

Using an easy-to-understand, how-to approach, this chapter teaches readers how to make their work interesting and effective.

Chapter 17: FUEL YOUR PASSION
Get started now!

This summary chapter motivates readers to fuel their passion for writing and persevere with their projects.

PART V: MAKE A NAME FOR YOURSELF

Chapter 18: MARKETING SAVVY THAT WORKS
Take what you've written and promote yourself!

This final chapter provides some of the most insightful information in this book: how to market books and how to use books to market the professional consultant, speaker, or trainer. Most of the marketing tips come from Tony Alessandra, whose marketing efforts have propelled him into the top echelons of the sales training and professional speaking worlds.

SPECIAL FEATURES

After the organization section, present the sales-oriented features that make your book particularly attractive. The need to write this section will force you to discover and/or create your book's special features. What does your book do for the reader? How does it uniquely accomplish its goals? What makes you qualified to write it? These and other issues are addressed in this section. Our example follows:

---

1.   Written in a light, conversational style that helps understanding and digestibility.

2.   Contains an abundance of useful examples and tips that writers can adopt immediately.

3.   Provides practical strategies for today's business writer for managing the task of writing books and articles.

4.   Sells getting published as a business activity necessary for the building of a consulting practice or speaking career.

5.   Written by established business writers, one with a very high profile.

6.   Provides proven marketing strategies that lend themselves to any promotional budget.

CONCLUSION

The conclusion is an optional section that wraps up all the features and benefits into one last effort to sell the editor. Read the following example, and decide for yourself if a conclusion fits your style and the way you want to come across in your proposal.

---

1.   *Publish and Flourish—A Consultant's Guide* can be successfully marketed through bookstores, book clubs, and direct mail.

2.   Readers will appreciate the relevant, professional, and practical way the book addresses the problems they experience in trying to write.

3.   No other book on the market targets the readers for whom article and book writing is such an attractive and profitable opportunity—consultants, speakers, and trainers.

SAMPLE CHAPTER

After the conclusion, add the finished draft of the first chapter. Although the chapter need not be in its absolutely finished state, it should be close to the form in which it would appear in the book.

Many writers do not use the first chapter as a sample but choose one from the middle of the book's outline to give the editor a truly representative example. (Often a book's first chapter contains introductory discussions that repeat thematic material from the proposal.)

MISCELLANEOUS

After the sample chapter, it is a good idea to include any articles, brochures, advertisements, testimonials, photographs, or other collateral material that will help sell you. Avoid including articles more than two years old, and keep this section to a maximum of ten or so pages. You don't want to give the impression that you think you have to bend over backward to sell yourself. If you have one, include a video or audio cassette of a recent television interview or speech. If you have any published books under your belt, provide copies of these as well, together with sales figures.

The proper length of a book proposal is whatever it takes to sell your idea. The average length ranges from ten to twenty-five pages. In a long proposal, it is important to put the most salient material up front. The objective is to draw in the editor quickly and then support your claims with background and other details.

Writing a book proposal can be compared to auditioning for a play. The actor is asked to perform a monologue or scene and is hired based on that sample. If a publisher likes your work, you'll be given the chance to prove yourself. You may become a star.

SMALL STEPS TO SUCCESS

Work to Be Done	Deadline

1. Think of five good titles for your book. _____
2. Think of five subtitles. _____
3. Write a one-sentence synopsis of the book. _____
4. Write a one-page bio of yourself. _____
5. Write a theme section for the proposal. _____
6. Make a list of similar books on the market. _____
7. Write a rationale or marketing analysis for _____ your book; include comments on the competition.
8. Outline your book into chapter titles, and _____ describe each chapter with a paragraph.
9. List the special features of your book. _____
10. Wrap up your proposal with a conclusion. _____
11. Include your sample chapter. _____
12. Gather materials such as articles and brochures to supplement your sample chapter. _____
13. Give your proposal to an experienced writer _____ for feedback. If possible, show it to a literary agent.

Get Started on This List Today

11

THE VALUE OF
LITERARY AGENTS

Literary agents perform a valuable service for publishers and writers. For publishers, they run interference between editors and the public by screening out books and writers not ready to be considered for publication. Most new books flow into publishing houses through a pipeline supported by literary agents. Editors trust the judgment of agents and give their submissions preferential treatment. Unsolicited manuscripts—those submitted directly by writers—are often banished to less senior editors' "slush piles" for months before they are dusted off and given a cursory glance.

Literary agents have the writer's best interest at heart. A good working relationship with an agent can motivate a writer and open doors that would otherwise be sticky, if not completely shut. An agent should be like a business partner. The best relationship is based on trust and enthusiasm, not connections. When you give an agent the responsibility of representing your book, you trust him with the disposition of a project that may have taken years to complete. His handling of that responsibility could affect your career, income, lifestyle, and reputation for years to come.

Among the many duties an agent performs for clients are the following:

- Honestly critiques your book, idea, or proposal, which increases its chances of publication.
- Knows the book market, including editors who might be interested in your type of book.
- Knows the nature of different publishers—who promotes well, who is going broke, who is solvent, who is overstocked, and so on.
- Uses his connections to land a contract and then negotiates the terms of that contract.
- Commands more money for you than you could get for yourself.
- Acts as a liaison between you and your editor.
- Distributes royalties to you and your co-authors.
- Sells subsidiary rights, such as book serialization and paperback and other rights.
- Helps you bring your ideas to fruition, finds projects for you, and provides co-authors if necessary.

In short, good literary agents earn their commissions.

HOW AGENTS WORK

Literary agents are like salespeople. They are constantly trying to maximize their time by selling the best products they can get their hands on. Reputable agents work for free until your book is sold; then they get 15 percent of your advance and future royalties.

Beware of agents who want money up front. Some call such payments a "reading fee." Good agents read for free; questionable agents charge a fee. If you were to pay the fee and have your manuscript rejected, how would you know for certain it was read? When you have a project that an agent is excited about, he will be happy to represent you on spec based on the belief that your work is marketable. Additionally, he will be willing to assume the risk of spending time and money on your behalf. Healthy skepticism dictates that you avoid agents who are overly concerned about being compensated for their time and expenses.

THE AGENCY CONTRACT

When you first align yourself with an agent, you may be asked to sign a contract giving the agency the right to represent you. The contract spells out the commission structure, how your agent is to be compensated, and so on. There are two important clauses to be aware of. One will try to obligate you to the agency for an unreasonable length of time. The other will try to lay claim to a percentage of your income from anything you produce within that contracted time. Some agents will ask for exclusive representation for two years; that's 15 percent of *all* your writing income, including income from work *they haven't sold for you*. If you were to write for a local magazine or newspaper, they would be entitled to a cut of that money, too.

Forget it! Change the contract so it applies only to a specific book for a reasonable length of time. Include a clause that lets you out of the contract after six months if the agent hasn't sold your book. If an agent hasn't found a publisher in that time, he never will. You have to be free to take your book elsewhere for more productive representation.

In the contract, don't give your agent an exclusive on your future work. Negotiate each contract on a book-by-book basis. An agent who insists on representing future books before selling your first one should be regarded suspiciously.

HOW TO GET AN AGENT

If your book or proposal is original, well positioned, and salable, getting an agent will be easy.

The best way to find an agent is through a personal referral— a colleague or friend who already has an agent. Ask him to recommend you to the agent, and the door will immediately be opened. Agents also prefer to find new clients this way.

If that fails, look in your home town for an experienced agent who has connections in New York City. Ask around as you would if you were shopping for a good doctor or an accountant.

If there is no one in your town who can instill confidence, go to the library and consult the *Literary Market Place*. (You can order a copy from R. R. Bowker, 1180 Avenue of the Americas, New York, New York, 10036.) This book lists reputable agents, the kinds of books or clients they are looking for, and their submission require-ments (for example, every agent wants you to submit a query with a self-addressed, stamped envelope).

After you have done some research, write a query letter to the agent(s). Describe your book idea, present your background and expertise, and ask if he might be interested in it. The query letter is important, so craft it carefully. It is your agent's first impression of your writing ability and overall professionalism.

Be persistent, and do not get discouraged if you are rejected. Different agents have different tastes and visions. Keep submitting your query letter until you find someone who responds positively.

Avoid multiple simultaneous submissions. Most agents will not spend the time reading your proposal or book if they know you are shopping around. No one wants to invest time and then be pre-empted by another agent. The only time you can get away with this strategy is when you have a book that is so hot that agents respond quickly to try to sign you up.

THE REVERSE APPROACH

There is an easy way to get an agent, but it is a long shot: submit your work directly to publishers and find one who will give you a contract. At that point, ask the editor to recommend an agent, or approach agents on your own. Few agents will turn down an author who has an interested publisher waiting in the wings.

If you submit your work to a publisher and it is turned down with an upbeat, encouraging letter, ask the editor to recommend an agent. If he liked your work, he will be happy to refer you to someone.

One last approach is worth mentioning: writers' conferences. If one is held in your town, take the time to attend. You will learn a great deal about writing and marketing books, and you will meet editors and agents scouting for new talent. You may not spend the time necessary to establish a rapport with an agent, but exchanging business cards is a good first step. Exposure is the name of the game.

THE AGENT QUERY LETTER

All of the principles that apply to article queries (covered in Chapter 5) also apply to agent queries. There are some additional tips to keep in mind.

Never (almost) call an agent. The only time you can justify a call is when your idea is so timely that it will go stale quickly. "Mr. Agent, I'm a reporter for a small newspaper. I just returned from the Middle East where I was held captive for three months and would like to write a book about my experience."

Always send a self-addressed stamped envelope.

Keep the query to no more than two pages. One page plus a table of contents works well.

Excite the agent with your style and content. Write a lively, humorous (if relevant), and upbeat letter.

Show that you've done your homework. Give proof of your book idea's salability. Show an awareness of your competition.

Describe your credentials in a positive light. You may be a first-time author, but you can highlight your consulting, training, or speaking career. Don't start with, "I've never written a book before, but . . ."

Be professional. Send your letter on good stationery. Use the proper salutation. Find out the agent's full name and its proper spelling. Never write, "To Whom It May Concern."

Include the essentials. Who you are. Why you would be a valuable client. What your book is about. The proposed length of your book. The ways that your book is different from (and similar to) the competition. Your qualifications for writing the book. Your writing credentials, including published articles and books, if any.

Start strong. A captivating lead-in sentence is a must. It doesn't matter if you start dramatically, funny, or businesslike, but do it with impact. "For sixty-seven days, I was locked in a tiny bathroom in a house in Baghdad, my captors threatening to torture me to death; weak, ragged, and hungry, I finally outsmarted them to escape and tell about it." Compare that to, "I was in Baghdad during Operation Desert Storm."

Be modest. Don't hype your idea or writing style. It's acceptable to compare your writing to that of a famous author, but be careful. Avoid gushing, as in, "My book will evoke endless belly-laughs and can be compared to Woody Allen's *Without Feathers*, though my book will be more sophisticated."

Be a perfectionist. Proofread, proofread, and then proofread your letter. Strive for zero defects. No typos, spelling errors, or grammatical goofs should escape your critical eye.

Avoid sounding desperate. Sell your confidence and emphasize your book's merits. Do not unload your emotional baggage or speculate about the consequences of failing to get your book published.

HOW AGENTS MAKE DECISIONS

Editors prefer to work with agents rather than writers because agents are more realistic than inexperienced writers. Writers tend to be eccentric, moody, and difficult to deal with, especially when it comes to money. How would you feel if you had spent two years writing a book and a publisher told you, "Your book is fantastic. We'll give you a contract, but your advance will only be a reimbursement of the postage you spent to mail it to us . . . Okay, okay, we'll also reimburse you for photocopies."

Although an agent negotiates in your behalf, he will not make decisions for you. On the contrary, *you*, with his help, will make all the decisions on the basic terms of your contract. The agent simply acts as your business consultant, liaison, and contract negotiator.

A good agent will explain what you can reasonably expect at this stage of your writing career so you will not feel exploited or underpaid by the publisher. Part of choosing an agent is finding someone you can trust. So believe your agent when he tells you not to expect a $50,000 advance.

Most agents are honest and conscientious. If your book is a good one, you have everything to gain by using an agent. The desire to do everything yourself to save 15 percent commission is petty and self-defeating in the long run. An agent can get you at least 15 percent more than you can get yourself.

An agent may also be instrumental in developing future projects. You might receive a telephone call one day that goes like this: "Joe, I just read an article that suggested a book idea to me, and I think you would be the ideal person to write it. If you want to put together a proposal, I know someone at Tripleday who would be interested in it."

The book business is like any other; there's always a middleman. When you consider the incredible number of books being submitted, rejected, accepted, and published each year, the odds of your book's being noticed without an agent become minuscule. The middleman is a necessary part of the business. Find one.

SMALL STEPS TO SUCCESS

Work to Be Done   **Deadline**

1. Ask colleagues, writers, or editors to recom-   _____
   mend an agent.
2. If Step 1 fails, use the *Literary Market Place* to   _____
   make a list of New York agents.
3. Write a succinct query letter about your book   _____
   idea.
4. Contact several agents, and find one who will   _____
   talk to you about your book idea.

Get Started on This List Today

12

PUBLISHING OPTIONS

Unpublished writers around the world have the same dream at least twice each night: a big, prestigious New York publishing house to turn their novels into best-sellers. Welcome to fame, fortune, Geraldo, Donahue, Oprah, *People* magazine, and the Betty Ford Clinic.

Although that fantasy motivates many writers, it is one you can live without. Becoming a celebrated writer is not the primary purpose for writing a book. You will use your books as marketing tools. Fame and fortune come through doing what you do best, which probably is not writing.

Do you need to get published by a big, prestigious New York publishing house? The answer depends on your values, patience, time frame, finances, ego, and many other factors. On the negative side, self-publishing will require you to exert more of a promotional effort, taking time or help away from your primary business. It will require storage, shipping, and handling of books. On the positive side, self-publishing will accelerate the submission-acceptance-rejection-production phases and provide you with more per-book profit.

Why would you consider a publishing house over self-publishing? One reason is prestige. It is quite rewarding (and carries more clout) to be able to say your book was published by John Wiley & Sons, Doubleday, or Simon & Schuster. Another reason is their wider distribution and promotion network. If you have a truly hot book, a publisher will distribute and promote it more effectively than you can. Your dreams of seeing your book in the local bookstore and being on the "Today Show" would come true. Even if your book is not destined for the best-seller lists, a publisher will still get it into more bookstores than you would.

Self-publishing is an option that is well worth considering. It is less prestigious but more practical for many people. There is no question that some books would never be published if they were not self-published. Why waste six months or a year submitting your manuscript to large publishers when you can self-publish and have the book working for you in a fraction of the time.

THE PUBLISHING BUSINESS

When you are considering self-publishing, ask yourself if you are willing and able to enter the publishing business because that is exactly what you will be doing. After the manuscript is written, you will remove your writer's hat and don your business hat. You will be dealing with graphic artists, printers, typesetters, illustrators, photographers, professional and trade associations, and possibly distributors and bookstore owners. You will be launching a new business in which you create, produce, and market a product. It's not a small task. You will take all the risk but also enjoy more of the profits.

Many writers who intend to self-publish get carried away with the propsect of being a published writer. They spend more money than necessary on the book's production and begin their publishing business with a low profit margin.

There are two ways to look at your publishing venture. One way is to consider the book a product that must be produced cheaply and distributed profitably. The other way is to see your book as an expensive promotional tool that you will use to stimulate your primary business. From this point of view, the book's profitability becomes secondary. Hopefully, most books will bring in business that will more than compensate you for the book's cost. Of course, a happy medium between the first way and the second would work well.

The decision to self-publish should be made with more than a modicum of realism. Many writers fall prey to selective anticipation and glamor blindness. Throughout the writing and production phases, their only vision is of the completed book. They fantasize about giving signed copies to their friends, talking about it at parties, and all the other ego-gratifying activities. What they fail to focus on are the demands of having to promote and market 1,000 to 5,000 books. They forget that on the glorious day when the printer has finished the books, they will have at least twenty boxes of books stacked up in their garages. How glamorous is that? It's glamorous only if you have set in motion the means to sell them.

COMPUTER-AIDED PUBLISHING

The computer is revolutionizing the publishing industry and making self-publishing less expensive every day. Developments in hardware and software have eliminated many of the services that must be farmed out to professionals. These days you can write your manuscript, add graphics, and design, typeset, and lay out your book with desktop publishing software. Add a laser printer to the system, and you could print out each book page and give it to your printer camera ready.

With a less expensive computer system, you could write and edit your manuscript and submit it to a typesetter on floppy disks. This would save you the expense of having your book entered manually into their typesetting computer. Eliminating this step will save you thousands of dollars and weeks of time.

SELF-PUBLISHING AND SHELF LIFE

Most trade books fizzle out within the first year of their lives, mostly due to insufficient promotion by publishers. Distributing books to bookstores is not enough to ensure success.

A self-publisher who puts the time and money into promotion can keep a book alive and selling well for years. Remember that the book serves two purposes. As a brochure, it brings in consulting and training jobs and speeches. As a profit center, it generates passive income.

If you are sufficiently motivated, the risk you take when self-publishing will turn into an asset rather than a liability. The more you have invested in your book, the harder you will work to get copies out of the garage.

One self-publishing success story that you may be familiar with is *The One-Minute Manager* by Ken Blanchard and Spencer Johnson. While developing the book, they printed copies, used them in their seminars, and refined the book based on feedback from their seminar participants. After five revisions and sales of 20,000 copies, they were in a strong position to take it to a publisher, who turned it into a phenomenal best-seller.

The decision to seek a publishing house or to self-publish brings into play one's ego, finances, professional standing, and goals. The checklists in Figure 12.1 will make you aware of the advantages and disadvantages of both options.

Evaluate each feature on the list on a scale from -3 to $+3$. For positive ratings, have the numbers stand for "advantage" ($+1$), "big advantage" ($+2$), and "major advantage" ($+3$). Do the same for the disadvantages: rate them from -1 to -3 to signify "minor disadvantage" (-1), "big disadvantage" (-2), and "major disadvantage" (-3). The sum of the scores will show you which avenue makes the most sense for you. Try to be objective in your ratings.

Regardless of your totals and your feelings on the matter, the best approach—from a time-management standpoint—is to write a book proposal and a sample chapter, find a literary agent to submit the proposal to publishers, wait and hope to land a contract, and write the book only after you've been given a contract.

If your belief in the salability of your book is unshakable, don't stop after submitting a proposal. Write the rest of the book. Then if you get a contract, your work will be finished. If you don't get a contract, you always have the option of self-publishing the completed manuscript or submitting it elsewhere.

TIPS FOR SELF-PUBLISHING

Assuming you have evaluated the pros and cons and decided to self-publish, here are some hints to smooth the way and increase your probability of success:

PUBLISHING HOUSE

More prestige   _____
More professional credibility   _____
No out-of-pocket expenses or risks   _____
They handle marketing and promotion   _____
More publicity possible, but not guaranteed   _____
Advance on royalties   _____
Often need a literary agent to break in   _____
Time-consuming (6 months to 2 years)   _____
Book must be original or well-positioned   _____
Often need to write book proposal   _____
Creates a deadline (stress) if proposal is accepted   _____
Rejection rate is high   _____
Some loss of artistic control   _____
Less profit margin for you   _____
                                            TOTAL = _____

SELF-PUBLISHING

Less prestige   _____
Slightly less credibility   _____
Substantial risk of capital   _____
You promote/market book (requires time and money)   _____
Money comes in only when books sell   _____
Higher profit margin   _____
No literary agent needed   _____
Less originality or positioning needed   _____
Faster turnaround time   _____
No book proposal needed   _____
100 percent artistic control   _____
100 percent business control   _____
No deadlines imposed   _____
                                            TOTAL = _____

Figure 12.1

- Target your book to a specific audience, preferably one you can reach by direct mail and other finely focused marketing techniques.
- Gear the book for an upscale market that can afford to pay a higher-than-usual price for your knowledge. Direct marketing requires a large profit margin.
- Consider the tax advantages of self-publishing. There are many write-offs to take advantage of, so consult an accountant or tax expert.
- Before your cartons of books are stacked up in the garage, read how-to books on marketing and direct mail advertising. Then plan your promotion and marketing campaign and follow through.
- Evaluate the expense and effectiveness of all the ways to market your book. With your unique strengths and industry exposure in mind, consider selling it:
  —From the speaking platform or in training and consulting programs.
  —Through other consultants, trainers, or speakers.
  —By direct mail.
  —In professional journal display ads.
  —Directly to corporations and associations.
  —In bookstores.
  —Through word of mouth.
  —At trade shows and conventions.
- Find a printer that specializes in books and has state-of-the-art equipment. Get estimates from several printers, both local and out of town. Printing estimates vary significantly.
- Changes in the book's contents are much less expensive if made before the pages are typeset. Take the time to read and edit your book carefully before rushing it into production.
- Be sure to get permission to print anything that has been published elsewhere. The last thing you need is a lawsuit.
- Create a press name, and print it on the binding of your book. Choose a professional-sounding name. Avoid using your last name. Something like "Regal" or "Apex Publishing" sounds better than "Homespun Press" or "Backyard Press." Tony used "Keynote Publishing" when he published *People Smart*.

- Register your book. Copyright Form TX and its instructions are available at your local library and directly from the U.S. Copyright Office:

    U.S. Copyright Office
    Library of Congress
    Washington, DC 20559

- Get an International Standard Book Number (ISBN), the number used for computerized cataloging of your book. Write for an ISBN System User's Manual:

    ISBN Agency
    c/o R. R. Bowker
    205 East 42d Street
    New York, New York 10017

- Reserve a space in *Books in Print*. Fill out an Advanced Book Information (ABI) Form, obtained from the ABI Department of R. R. Bowker.

- To get the best price, plan your printing for times when printers are slow (summer or middle of the winter).

Self-publishing won't get you on the best-seller list, but it will get your book into the hands of prospective clients. For many writers, this is the only reason needed to justify self-publishing. In the long run, the career advantages of being an author will far outweigh the minor detail of how your book was published.

SMALL STEPS TO SUCCESS

Work to Be Done   **Deadline**

1. Go through the checklists in this chapter to   _____
   determine your publishing preference.

2. Obtain a copyright application.   _____

3. Send away for the forms for an ISBN number   _____
   and an Advanced Book Reservation Form.

4. Talk to colleagues who have self-published   _____
   for their impressions of the advantages and
   disadvantages.

5. Choose a name for your publishing company.   _____

Get Started on This List Today

13

BOOK CONTRACTS:
CAVEAT SCRIPTOR!

The most exciting moment in a writer's life is when the telephone rings and an editor or literary agent is on the other end offering a book contract. Suddenly all the hard work is beginning to pay off.

If you have an agent, you will enjoy the luxury of having someone else negotiate the contract for you. If you do not have an agent, a general understanding of book contracts is imperative.

In your light-headed state during that magic call, you might be tempted to agree to anything the editor offers. Since this editor has truly made your day, you may expect that he also has your best interests at heart. He does, but he also has to cut the best deal possible for his company. Remember, to the editor, your book deal is merely another business call. Sorry to burst your bubble, but you will need to balance elation with equanimity when your moment of glory comes. So go to bat for yourself.

Do not agree to anything during the initial call. The editor will mention the amount of the advance and the royalty rate and tell you a standard contract will be sent to you. At that point, ask for a boilerplate contract—that is, a contract with no numbers filled in. Don't be intimidated by anything he says to imply the contract is inflexible. Tell the editor you cannot sign a contract until your lawyer or an agent has reviewed it. Be sure to assure him that you are interested in striking a mutually beneficial deal and will call in a few days to discuss details. He will understand and let you off the hook. Then hang up the phone and throw a party. After you have recuperated, do your homework and prepare yourself for negotiating.

THE PUBLISHER'S CONTRACT

The typical contract for a first-time writer offers the maximum advantage to the publisher. You are in a weak negotiating position with your first book. You will be anxious to get the book published and may concede anything to the publisher. They know this euphoric state is common, especially among first-time authors, and will use it to their best business advantage.

Experienced writers and literary agents know that all contracts are negotiable. When working without an agent, however, neophytes go to one extreme or the other; they either sign the contract without reading it, or consult an attorney to try to change every clause in the document. Don't go crazy; find a compromise between these two extremes.

When the contract arrives, read it over as many times as necessary to understand it. Make notes on what you would like changed. There are some excellent books on the subject, among them, *How to Be Your Own Literary Agent* by Richard Curtis (Houghton Mifflin, 1984), and *Negotiating a Book Contract* by Mark Levine (Moyer Bell Limited, 1988). You can also use your publisher as a resource. Call your editor or the publisher's contracts department for explanations.

Publishers' contracts contain between 15 and 100 clauses. To discuss the interpretation and negotiation of an entire contract comprehensively would require a 200-page chapter. Our discussion here will be limited to the major areas of contention that arise for first-time authors. This introduction will increase your awareness but not make you an instant expert. To become an expert, consult an expert.

There are some standard clauses and provisions to negotiate with your editor. Remember that the first draft of the contract will be written to their advantage, so ask for the changes you want.

THE ADVANCE

The advance and royalty rate are generally discussed over the telephone, with the finer details handled in writing. In case you are not clear on what an advance is, it is money the publisher pays you up front, before the book is published, to help you with expenses while you are writing the book. The advance is money paid to you *against* royalties, *not a bonus paid in addition to royalties*. It is a demonstration of the publisher's faith in your book's marketability, which is why most advances are so low. (Let's face it; fifty thousand books are published in the United States each year. Only a fraction of them are best-sellers.) When your book hits the bookstores and starts selling, you will not receive any further payments until it has sold enough copies to reimburse the publisher for your advance.

Every writer fantasizes about receiving a substantial advance, especially after reading about celebrities who have received million-dollar advances. Unfortunately, the nonfiction book you will write and the best-sellers cranked out by Stephen King are light-years apart. The range of advance money for a first-time author of a nonfiction trade book is between $500 and $10,000, with the average being between $3,000 and $5,000.

When negotiating an advance, keep in mind that editors do have some leeway. They always offer the low end of their range. Ask for twice as much, and be prepared to accept less. Play the game. Pretend you are in Tijuana haggling over a black velvet painting.

Publishers are generally not in a hurry to pay the advance. When you get paid depends on the size of the advance and how complete your book is at the time of the negotiation.

The most common payout is half of the advance upon the signing of the contract and the other half when you deliver an acceptable finished manuscript. Some contracts stipulate that the second half of the advance will be paid upon publication of the book. Don't buy it, especially if your advance is small to average. Publication will be a year or more after manuscript completion; you certainly don't want to wait that long. In addition, if the publisher were to decide not to publish your book after all, you would not receive the balance of the advance. Be sure to change this clause so you will be paid when you deliver the manuscript.

When a book is sold as a proposal, the payout will often be

one-half upon signing the contract, one-quarter on the submission of half of the book, and the balance on the acceptance of the completed manuscript.

ROYALTIES

The standard royalty rate will be virtually impossible to change for your first book. These will vary somewhat by publisher and will usually be built into the contract. A typical royalty might be 10 percent of the publisher's receipts; others may offer a percentage of the retail price. You might try to ask for "escalators," which would bump up the royalty rate at certain sales points—usually 5,000 copies.

Trade paperback royalties are less; they begin at 6 to 7½ percent and move up to 9 or 10 percent. There are some variations to these figures. You might be able to lower the first escalator from 5,000 books to 3,500 and the second cutoff from 10,000 to 7,000. This is where a good agent is helpful. After your first book, you will have much more negotiating power regarding royalty rates.

THE COPYRIGHT

Under the 1978 copyright law, your manuscript is considered to be copyrighted as soon as you write it; therefore, you do not have to register and copyright it formally. Nevertheless, you should register your work in case you ever have to go to court to prove the work is yours. If you've gotten a book contract, don't worry about a thing. Publishers take care of copyright registration.

The copyright should always be registered in your name, not the publisher's. If the contract mentions the renewal of the copyright, it is an old contract, and the renewal clause should be deleted. Under the current copyright law, renewal is no longer necessary.

DELIVERY DATES

The publisher will specify a deadline by which you have to complete and deliver an "acceptable" manuscript. Editors are familiar with writers' habits—good and bad—and will often specify a deadline that is two or three weeks before the actual date that the book *must* be in their hands. Before you assume you have this leeway, talk to your editor, and make sure it exists.

Ask for an extension if you need it. It's better to have too much time and deliver early than to be unreliable and continually asking for extensions. Request an extension at least two months before the deadline, and get the approval in writing. In your letter of request, describe your progress, and give responsible reasons for needing more time. Publishers are accustomed to dealing with writers who procrastinate or become blocked; they will be reasonable. If your manuscript is not delivered after numerous extensions, the publisher has the right to void the contract and request the advance be returned.

"ACCEPTABLE MANUSCRIPT"

Every contract mentions the phrase "acceptable manuscript." This clause gives the publisher the right to reject your book later for no other reason than it is judged to be "unacceptable." If you get a contract on a completed manuscript, this will not apply unless you completely foul up requested revisions, which is unlikely.

There are legitimate and illegitimate reasons for the rejection of a book after it has been delivered. The legitimate reasons commonly given are that the book was poorly written, inadequately researched, or delivered too late. It is difficult to know when a legitimate reason is simply an excuse to cover the publisher's change of heart. Publishers change their minds for a number of reasons: market trends or corporate policies may change, the editor who went to bat for your book may have left the company, or a competing book may have appeared on the market.

The most frequent reason for invoking the "unacceptable manuscript" clause is late delivery. Given that many books are written to take advantage of a fad, a late delivery means the entire market appeal has evaporated. With late delivery, the publisher is justified in rejecting the book and demanding the return of the advance.

If you are in the unfortunate position of having your book rejected as unacceptable by a publisher, you have several options. If you believe the reasons are sincere but not well founded, talk to the editor. See if you can iron out your differences. If you cannot, you have two choices. The better one is to find another publisher. The other is to hire an attorney and fight for the retention of your advance, although you will spend more on legal fees than the advance is worth. If the advance is substantial and worth fighting for, remember to confine the legal battle to the issue of the advance, not the publishing of the book. You don't want to fight for publication. A publisher who is forced to publish a book will treat it as an outcast and fail to promote it adequately.

If a publisher asks you to refund the advance, the common practice is to repay it *if and when* you sell the book to another publisher. If the editor demands the money immediately and there seems to be no room to negotiate, consult an attorney. A stern telephone call from your attorney may encourage the publisher to back down or settle out of court.

NUMBER OF WORDS

In your contract you will agree to an approximate number of manuscript words. This is important. Your editor wants to know what he's buying in terms of size so the book can be priced accordingly. Price and size help your editor position your book in the publisher's catalog, so you must deliver what you promise. Keep in mind that the average manuscript page has about 250 words.

SUBSIDIARY RIGHTS

Subsidiary rights include first serialization rights (republication in magazines of excerpts from your book); paperback and book club rights; British and foreign translation rights; motion picture, television, and audio/video rights; and so on. An agent will attempt to retain all the subsidiary rights for you. If you don't have an agent, the publisher will retain most of the rights and split the proceeds with you when these rights are sold.

The standard split for subsidiary rights is between 50-50 and 80-20. Fight for the audio/video and electronic rights. After all, the next step after publishing your book is to make an audiotape album. Wouldn't you hate to give the publisher 50 percent of your income! It makes more sense for you to retain those rights.

The whole issue of rights and splits becomes complicated. If you get as far as landing a book contract, either spend the time reading the books we have recommended or consult a literary agent or entertainment lawyer. A good agent will be able to read a contract with an experienced eye. He will also have a set of variations to the boilerplate contract that will shift the advantage in some clauses to the author.

WARRANTY AND INDEMNIFICATION

This clause is also known as the author's guarantee. In essence, you must guarantee that you have the right to sell the book to the publisher, the book was written by you and not plagiarized, and permission has been obtained for all copyrighted material used in the book. This clause protects the publisher from any lawsuits that may arise due to charges of slander, libel, plagiarism, or obscenity.

This clause may seem unfair, but it is virtually impossible to remove from the contract. Although publishers are protected by insurance, it does not cover the author. A lawsuit could financially ruin a writer, whereas a publishing house is better able to absorb the loss. Despite their advantage, publishers insist that this clause remain in the contact.

There is only one thing you can do to guarantee you will never be sued for libel: never say anything. Once your words become public in any way, you may be open to lawsuits at any time. To lessen the chances that your words will not cause legal problems, consult an entertainment lawyer about controversial parts of the text, or have the publisher read the book with an eye toward libel, plagiarism, or whatever your concern is.

TERMINATION CLAUSE

If this clause is properly written, it will allow you to retrieve all rights if and when the publisher lets your book go out of print or fails to reprint the book within six months. If the publisher has licensed your book to another publisher but it has not appeared on the market yet, you cannot invoke this clause. For example, your publisher may let the hardcover edition go out of print after selling the paperback rights to another publisher. During the lag period before the paperback appears, your book would still be considered alive, albeit temporarily out of sight. If your book is a hot item, the lag time will be nonexistent or brief.

PUBLISHER'S DETERMINATION

The publisher has the right to determine what it will do with your book. This means the publisher decides on the format, how the book will be printed, where and how it will be promoted, the list price, the cover design, the number of copies in the first printing, and the title. This is what is meant by losing control of your book.

It is unlikely a publisher would force a new title on an author. If the publisher wants a better title, your editor will ask for some new possibilities and suggest some. A new title is generally agreed upon by all parties.

If an author has some compelling reasons why the book should be designed or promoted a certain way, a publisher will listen. Both of you have the same goal in mind, so unless your ideas are invalid or expensive, the publisher may accommodate you. Always ask for what you want.

FREE COPIES

Imagine your book is being published. You can't wait to send auto-graphed copies to all your friends and relatives. The question arises, Will you have to buy those copies? The answer depends on how many literate relatives you have. Most publishers give the author between six and fifty books. They will generally offer to sell books to you at about a 40 percent discount. When negotiating your con-tract, try to get copies at a 50 percent discount or better.

A discount is especially important to consultants, speakers, and trainers. You would be wise to buy large quantities of books to sell at a profit or give away for promotional purposes. If you guarantee the publisher you will buy a large quantity (1,000 or more) of every press run, you may be able to negotiate up to a 75 percent discount. Of course, there would be no returns and no royalties generated, but those conditions are reasonable.

When dealing with small publishers, it is difficult to get a sub-stantial advance. An alternative to accepting an insultingly low ad-vance is to ask for books in lieu of money. Ask for the dollar amount of the advance in books *at the publisher's cost.* You can later turn those books into cash or use them for promotion. A good example of this is the deal Tony Alessandra was able to negotiate for the revised edition of *Non-Manipulative Selling* (Simon & Schuster, 1987). He and Phil Wexler, one of his co-authors, received 1,000 books each with no deduction from the royalties in lieu of an advance. The 2,000 books are, in effect, a bonus for signing the contract since they will not have to be paid for out of royalties.

PUBLISHER'S REVISIONS

Somewhere in the contract, the publisher may attempt to reserve the right to edit and alter the book. This does not mean simply correcting typos and grammar; it may mean freedom for substantial rewriting. Change this clause, or insert something to this effect: "Such editing will not change the meaning or alter the text of the work or its title without the consent of the author."

Remember that you are the one at risk for libel and plagiarism charges, so you have to insist on the right to review the changes made by the publisher. If the editor balks at your resistance, ask the publisher to assume all responsibility for libel and plagiarism. Most likely this tactic will help them see your point of view.

OPTIONS CLAUSE

The publisher's contract often has a clause giving it the right of first refusal of your next book. In other words, the publisher wants the exclusive right to be the first to consider buying your next work. This clause should be deleted entirely; it could hinder your freedom in the future.

If your first book was well promoted and made money for you, you may want to give your next book to the same publisher. If your book did not sell or you were dissatisfied with the way you were treated by the publisher, you will want to look elsewhere. The options clause does not force the publisher to publish a book it doesn't want, but it forces the author to submit the book to a publisher he may otherwise reject. The publisher's offer, however, does not have to be accepted.

If the publisher insists on keeping the options clause, have a time limit imposed. Add something to this effect: "The publisher shall have 60 days in which to accept or refuse the book or proposal. Failure to respond within that time shall constitute a refusal."

ADVERTISING BUDGET

A clause that stipulates a minimum advertising budget is a difficult one to write into a contract. Unless you have an impressive track record or celebrity status, the publisher will not consider a clause offering you any promotional guarantees. You can expect to be told not to worry and that it is in their best interest to advertise your book. In reality, publishers follow the 80-20 rule: 80 percent of the advertising budget goes to 20 percent of the book list. Your first book will likely not be among that 20 percent.

One recommended tactic is to conduct market research on your own before you get to the contract stage; then identify for the publisher the specific ideal markets for direct-mail advertising. Generate a list of magazines, professional journals, and newsletters for yourself and your publisher. You will need the list for submitting articles; your publisher will need the list for placing display ads and sending books to be reviewed.

GRANT IN AID

Some publishers help defray writing costs, such as manuscript typing, computer searches, travel, and research assistance. You might get the publisher to lease a computer for you. Even if you do all the typing yourself, it pays to ask the publisher to cover some expenses. Grants of this sort are made only in situations in which you land a contract based on a proposal and sample chapters. If you submit a completed manuscript, don't expect to be reimbursed for expenses.

Contracts change constantly and must be dealt with on a case-by-case basis. The awareness you have gained from the discussion in this chapter will serve as a starting point from which you can expand your knowledge. Writers who are inclined to learn more about contracts fare better during negotiations than those who are uniformed.

After you have published your first book, one excellent way to keep abreast of the profession is to join the Author's Guild. For information, the address is 234 West 44th Street, New York, New York 10036.

If you have taken the time and expended the effort to write a book, you owe it to yourself to familiarize yourself with book contracts. Become an expert, but make yourself a reasonable expert. Know what the various clauses mean, implicitly and explicitly, but do not become unrealistic. You are a first-time author; there is just so much you can get for an average book.

We wish you the best of luck in having many contracts to negotiate.

SMALL STEPS TO SUCCESS

Work to Be Done   **Deadline**

1. Reread and study this chapter.   _____
2. Buy and read one of the recommended books.   _____
3. Contact an agent or publisher, and ask for a   _____
   copy of a standard contract.

Get Started on This List Today

PART FOUR

Develop The Skills Of A Successful Writer

14

STYLE: ADDING PANACHE TO YOUR POINT

In many ways, written and verbal communications are like music. Good speakers and writers make their sentences ebb and flow by choosing their words carefully and controlling the pace, rhythm, and volume of the delivery. They create excitement by building crescendos, crashing cymbals, and pounding drums. These musical qualities serve to draw in, pump up, relax, and move the listener/reader emotionally. The result is writing or speaking with style and impact.

Bad communicators offend your senses with sour notes and nonsequiturs, or they lull you to sleep with monotony. In the editing and rewriting phase of your writing, read your work with an eye toward cleaning it up and creating a style that works for you rather than against you.

SEVEN SIGNS OF EXCELLENT WRITING

Similar to the many genres of music, writing also has many styles. Regardless of the style, good writing always exhibits at least six of the seven signs of excellence. Always strive to:

1. Use brevity.
2. Strive for clarity.
3. Write with precision.
4. Harmonize with yourself.
5. Write for your reader.
6. Choose words that convey honesty.
7. Wax poetic.

Incorporate these principles into your writing and you will improve it significantly.

Use Brevity

When you edit your work, don't think of what you can add; think of what you can delete. In nonfiction, tight writing is the best writing. (This is also true of screen and playwriting, where every word should advance the plot.) Digressions, anecdotes, humorous asides, and philosophical conjectures are informative and entertaining *in moderation*. Do not be like the speaker who shortchanges his audience by giving more laughs than content. Serve your reader meat and potatoes, not just dessert.

One way to write with brevity is to have a strong focus. Writing without a specific point of view produces dull material that lacks readability and credibility. If you were to write an article on nutrition, you would have to discuss everything from A to Zinc to cover it fairly. If, however, your title were "The Effects of Sugar on Hyperactive Children," you would have a manageable subject that could be written with brevity.

Once you have focused on a unique angle, include only information that is relevant. In the introduction of an article, avoid the common mistake of introducing the subject with a long, abstract overview. Book chapters have more leeway, but your introductions must still point in the direction you are headed. If you were writing about nutrition, you wouldn't begin with a recollection of your adolescent years when you sat in front of the television eating chocolate cake with a snow shovel. Write a short introduction, and then get into the body of the article or chapter. By the end of the first paragraph, you should be addressing your subject directly, not just alluding to it.

Know where you are going with your subject; avoid dancing around. Outline your piece before writing, and remember the principle of having a beginning, a middle, and an end.

Strive for Clarity

A good writer makes his meaning crystal clear—and quickly—by giving specific, useful facts and offering advice in a direct, cookbook style.

Avoid ambiguity by defining pronouns before using them. Refer to "he/she/it/his/her/their" only after telling the reader who or what you are talking about.

When you present a workshop, you repeat important points so your audience will remember. This teaching technique is valid for speaking and leading workshops but not for writing. Writers assume they have their readers' attention, so it is unnecessary to repeat key ideas as often. It *is* acceptable to refresh readers' memories later or, better, refer back to the original discussion.

In writing, it is unprofessional to state in advance what you are going to discuss. Speakers do it all the time, but it's boring to read, "This chapter will deal with styles of writing and include qualifiers, formal versus conversational writing, prescriptive versus descriptive styles, power and authority, first person versus third person" and so on. Just introduce the subject, and launch into the details.

Write with Precision

Precision, clarity, and brevity are closely related. Clarity is saying what you mean, precision is saying *exactly* what you mean, and brevity keeps it all short and to the point. A precise word can often replace a less precise phrase. Always strive to write and edit with an economy of words. A thesaurus or dictionary will help you achieve literary parsimony. Being precise etches a sharper image in your readers' minds, and it strengthens your credibility; you end up teaching more and confusing less.

Discussing one idea at a time increases your precision. A freight train of phrases in a sentence will only make it awkward and confusing. Instead of writing, "In the event of rain," write, "If it rains."

Rather than "due to the fact that . . ." say, "because." Delete "I believe that . . ." or "It is my opinion that . . ." and simply make your statement. We've all heard people say, "so and so is a *close personal friend* of mine." This is silly and redundant. Since when are people ever "close personal enemies" or "close impersonal friends"?

State statistics directly rather than generalizing about them first. It's better to say, "85 percent of the runners saw mirages" than, "In the desert heat, an overwhelming number of runners—more than expected—saw mirages. In fact, it was 85 percent."

Don't beat around the bush. Get right to the information you have uncovered in your research. Instead of saying, "Various ethnic groups have settled in New York," say, "New York is home to Greeks, Italians, Puerto Ricans, to name a few."

Harmonize with Yourself

As in a symphony, sudden changes in writing style can be dramatic and startling. Style changes done unintentionally or to excess stress readers and make them squirm. Readers "hear" dissonance when they encounter an inappropriate change in tense or person, a sudden change in point of view, or a grammatical faux pas. Harmony is achieved by maintaining consistency in mood, intellectual level, style, and punctuation.

Write for Your Reader

The best speakers customize their presentations to their audiences. An important part of reaching a readership is personalizing your article or book, that is, putting everything in terms that your intended audience will understand. For example, you would bore readers with an abstract discussion about "The Value of Communication in Sales." That's an article you would write if you were a college professor. A more personal article would be, "How to Make More Sales by Improving Your Communication Skills." Write directly to your audience, and you'll increase the odds that they'll read your work to the end.

Put humanity into everything you write. Writing about ideas is fine for some subjects, but whenever possible, write about people. Direct your ideas to the reader by occasionally saying "you."

The practice of putting yourself in your work in terms of "I" or "we" is highly debatable and depends on the type of book or article you are writing. Of course, the preference of your editor, if you have one, is important as well. Our preference is to write in the second person (you/your) or third person (he/she/they). We will, however, postpone discussing this until a later section, lest we digress and be accused of not following our own advice.

Choose Words That Convey Honesty

The best way to achieve honesty and sincerity in your writing is to be yourself. Don't fill up your work with esoteric references and twenty-five-cent words for the sake of impressing readers. Honesty is using the thesaurus to find words you already know, not words you've never seen. Be true to your natural writing style. Don't try to sound like Erma Bombeck or Andy Rooney if you don't think the way they do. Be yourself, and, if your message is worthwhile, readers will enjoy your work.

Being honest may seem like a strange suggestion to make. After all, how will readers know if you are being honest? They cannot see your body language or eye contact on the printed page—or can they? They can. Dishonest writing is soft, unconvincing, tentative, and noncommittal. It is marred by many of the flaws this chapter is teaching you to avoid.

Wax Poetic

After mastering the basics of writing, you can begin to be more creative. Good writing does not have to be good art, but it can be artistic with some extra thought. When reading other writers' work, jot down creative, poetic, or inspirational phrases that tickle your fancy. Be sure they are not clichés. The only thing worse than using a trite phrase is thinking it is new and clever. When you have a collection of literary gems, you can sprinkle them throughout your work (giving credit to the author, of course). For example, a conversation about a romantic relationship yielded this metaphor: "I'd hate to see you dashed upon the shores of her indifference." Such poetry! It evokes a powerful image of a ship running aground in a violent storm, the waves pounding her mercilessly, which is precisely how some people feel when they are emotionally shipwrecked. Compare that to the simple statement, "I'd hate to see you rejected by her." Big deal; anyone can write that.

WORDS AND MUSIC

Now that you know your words are supposed to sound like music, a brief course in composition is in order. It is not enough to read this section once. Keep these tips in front of you when you edit your work, and they will improve your style immensely.

Write As If You Were Speaking

You have the advantage of already being a communicative person. You have a well-trained ear for proper English. Now you have to transfer that ability to the written word.

An effective writer pleases readers by creating sentences that sound conversational. Remember to write as if you were composing a letter to a friend. This practice will loosen up your style and give your prose a familiar feeling. Writing conversationally also ensures that you will use everyday words that immediately convey their meanings. The best style is fluid, unstilted, relaxed, and reader friendly.

There is a paradox to writing conversationally. Inasmuch as you want your writing to sound conversational, it should not duplicate conversation. Remember precision, brevity, and clarity? They usually do not apply to conversations. Most conversations sound like this: "I had a great idea yesterday. I was sitting in the Forty-second Street deli, eating a pastrami sandwich; it was terrible, too much fat; I usually ask for lean cuts, but I forgot; anyway, I was looking at the neon sign in the window; you know, the one for Coors, and I noticed how dusty it was; it reminded me of my . . ." Hold it! That's *too* conversational.

Being conversational does not mean you are chatty or overly familiar. This example of a chatty style is appropriate only for used car salesmen: "Wanna buy a good used car? Hey, no problem! I'm the one who can show you how. Just keep reading." There is a fine line between being humorously loose in your "dialogue" with the reader and being chatty. There are parts of this book where the style becomes a little more loose for the sake of humor, but it never gets out of hand. Feel free to use this book as an example of good writing; then call us when you're looking for a used car.

The conversational style is appropriate for nonfiction books like this one and, most likely, the one you will write. A formal style that puts more distance between you and the reader is appropriate for academic pieces and some journal articles. When you begin to write articles for professional journals, be sure to read a few issues to determine their style.

Vary the Length of Sentences

One way to hold the reader's attention and sound conversational is to vary the lengths of your sentences. This sentence has five words. Five-word sentences are fine. But too many get dull. You can see for yourself. This is beginning to drone. When you vary the length of your sentences, you create waves of sound that keep readers alert. Short sentences are used for emphasis. Long sentences convey complex thoughts and often have more than one dependent clause. Used in moderation, both lengths are effective. When overdone, however, they become monotonous. Like this. Believe me. I've read them. Often. No joke. So the moral of the story is—use variety as a spice.

Use Different Sentence Constructions

Most sentences have a subject (*John*), a verb (*eats*), and an object (*quiche*), in that order. Like sentence length, this order should be varied. Start some sentences with dependent clauses such as, "Even at the age of thirty-eight, Ron participated in risky sports such as barefoot waterskiing." Another example of a dependent clause, which adds information in the middle of the sentence, is this sentence.

Experiment with Parallel Construction

Sometimes keeping the sentence construction the same will not bore the reader. It will emphasize the similarity of ideas being expressed or give them a poetic quality. Politicians and professional speakers do this all the time to drive home their points. You've heard it a thousand times: "There is sewage in the waters; there is pollution in the air; and there is rhetoric on the podium! Frankly, it is the latter that makes me sick."

Motivational speakers regularly use parallel construction as a tool: "So get up, get organized, and get writing! Create some excitement in your career!"

Use Complete Sentences

There are times when sentence fragments add impact, but typically they are unnecessary and amateurish. For a long time there has been a trend in popular fiction to disregard grammatical traditions by starting sentences with *and* or *but*. The practice is tolerable in moderation, but when overused, it becomes sloppy, lazy, and unprofessional, especially in business writing. And for those who know better, it makes reading the material annoying. But the final decision is yours.

After years of reading, readers expect to see a subject and verb. They listen for them. If they don't hear them often, they notice the omission as you would dead keys on a piano. Always give your readers complete sentences. They bought your book; the least you could do is give them a simple subject and verb.

Don't Repeat Uncommon Words

When you use common words like *and* and *the*, no one notices the repetition. If you were to write, "The speaker told an outrageous joke that only the outrageous people laughed at, and they did so outrageously," readers would notice the overuse and become outraged. Use a thesaurus or dictionary to find synonyms for key words, and your writing will stay fresh.

The same principle applies to writing copy for brochures, ads, and, especially, bios. When talking about someone, alternate the use of the person's name with the pronoun. An excerpt from one of Garry's bios is a good example. "Garry is a modern-day Renaissance man who brings his quick New York wit and cosmopolitan charm to everything he does, regardless of whether it's wanted. He attributes his gift for comedic one-liners to the prenatal influence of vaudeville. Garry's heroes are Neil Simon and Woody Allen, although the picture he kneels in front of every morning is his own."

Use the End of Sentences for Emphasis

Look back at the last sentence in the previous paragraph. Notice how the funny part of the sentence, "is his own," comes at the end. This was done intentionally to create the comedic impact. The end of a sentence has more emphasis than the beginning or middle. It is the last thing read and the first remembered. If you were to rearrange the last sentence of Garry's bio, it would lose its humor.

This tip will serve you well when you are writing business letters. In the following examples, notice how the order of words changes the emphasis.

"By June 1, please send me a check for $550."

"Please send me a check for $550 by June 1."

"By June 1, a check for $550 should be sent to me."

This is an important principle to apply to your consulting, speaking, and training as well. Your most powerful words should be placed at the end of sentences, and the primary message you want your audience to remember should be briefly reiterated immediately before you receive your standing ovation.

Use Powerful Words

Some words are mesmerizing. Some merely induce a mild trance, and others are so poorly chosen that the reader becomes fablungid. Consider what occurred in your mind just now. You were smoothly reading when suddenly you took a mental step back. You lost the flow because of the intrusion of an unfamiliar word, *fablungid*.

When editing, comb the manuscript for all words that could break the reader's flow. Good editing entails far more than merely searching for misspelled words and typos. Replace bizarre words with powerful ones.

Powerful words are short and to the point. For example, instead of saying *sexual assault*, you create impact with the word *rape*. *Stretch* is stronger than *extend*. *Rich* is more powerful than *wealthy*. *See* is stronger than *envision* or *imagine*. *Found* is better than *discovered*. *Fell* is better than *collapsed*. You get the idea. Use a thesaurus or dictionary to find better word choices than the ones that first came to mind.

Powerful sentences are specific. Notice the difference between "A man entered the room" and "A priest entered the room." The latter piques your interest. Being specific about your subjects is as important as using active instead of passive verbs (to be covered subsequently). Specificity gives your writing movement and holds the reader. Instead of saying *snake*, say *cobra*. Replace *talk* with *gossip*, *chat*, or *jabber*; substitute *powerful* for *strong*.

Powerful words are direct and honest. If you are writing about making a good first impression and are telling a story about a man wearing a bright-green polka-dotted tie, don't say, "He looked silly," say, "He looked like a clown." The only time you have to soften criticism is when you are talking face-to-face with the six-foot-four clown who wore the green polka-dotted tie. When you gossip to the rest of the world, however, go for the jugular.

Powerful words are subtle and varied. There are many ways to convey the same thought, so don't repeat yourself too often. If you are writing about ability, find other words to mix in. You can substitute *proficiency, competence, facility, efficiency, effectiveness*, and others. A command of the language adds credibility to everything you do.

Don't Insult Your Readers

As a professional who wants to be remembered, you use specific techniques to ensure your message will be heard and understood by your audience. You naturally slow down for emphasis, repeat important information, and describe concepts as simply as possible. These techniques are suitable for speaking, but they don't translate well to the written word. Worse, they insult your readers.

Listening has one set of demands; reading has another. Reading is a slower process, requiring more attention but less repetition and simplicity. It is unnecessary to give an example for every concept you present. More details don't always increase understanding, but they can rob your readers of the satisfaction of thinking for themselves.

Write with the assumption that your readers have had the same general life experiences as you. Furnish only the highlights, not all the details. Let readers fill in the rest. Write as if you were on the podium speaking with a time limit. That should save you from verbosity.

Use Words to Convey Enthusiasm

On the podium there are numerous verbal and nonverbal ways to convey enthusiasm. On paper you have to rely on your words. Don't put exclamation marks after important sentences. That's very amateurish. Instead, choose your words carefully. Remember, every sentence carries a different weight. It would be impossible and undesirable to give each sentence monumental importance. Both written works and speeches wax and wane in energy level.

Most adverbs and many adjectives are unnecessary. Instead of beefing up weak words, select words that pack a punch. For example, "He slammed the door" is better than "He angrily closed the door." When writing an anecdote and quoting dialogue, don't add adverbs after "he said"; let the nature of the dialogue evoke the emotion. Compare these two: "What are you doing?" he asked angrily. Better: "What the hell are you doing, Pal?" he asked.

Use the Active Voice

Readers are drawn in and held by words that do something, especially if they evoke mental images. For this reason, delete as many passive verbs as possible and replace them with active verbs.

Passive verbs are often compounded with verbs of "being," such as *is, was, are,* and *will be.* For example, replace *was running* with *ran, is planning to* with *plans to,* and *I was driving* with *I drove.*

Verbs of being that stand alone are also passive. Compare these two sentences: "The sailboats were anchored, their silhouettes reflected below them." "The sailboats stood on their reflections." The latter gives action (standing) to even the most tranquil scene, and it is more poetic.

The active voice combined with specific facts will sell your concept to readers more quickly. Listen to the difference in impact between, "You will be more successful" and "Increase your sales, earn more money, and gain recognition." The active voice defines exactly what you are talking about. Use it in your presentations as well.

Delete Qualifiers

Qualifiers are words that dilute the strength of your statements. They make a sentence sound tentative, conditional, and wishy-washy.

Qualifiers such as *I think, it appears that,* and *perhaps* are symptoms of a writer who is not willing to take a stand.

Assert yourself. Replace qualifiers with commands and positive statements. If you are recommending something controversial and want to temper your assertion by giving the reader a choice, come right out and say so: "This is a new, unorthodox approach that may not appeal to everyone. If you want to try it, take two tablespoons of desiccated bullfrog, add three pounds of milk-fed eastern rattlesnake livers, ½ clove garlic . . ." This tack is much stronger and self-assured than saying, "Your symptoms might respond to a new treatment, so you could try mixing . . ."

Qualifiers beat around the bush; at worst, they are dishonest. Never say, "He wore a bright-green tie and didn't quite make a good first impression," when your true thoughts were, "That bright-green tie made him look like a clown. He made a terrible first impression on all of us."

Use Third Person; Avoid First Person

Nonfiction books and articles should not be written in the first person (*I, me, mine*). Novels, love letters, and confessions are acceptable in the first person, but they'd better be interesting. Everything else should be written in the third person (*he, she, his, her, they, their, it*) or the second person (*you, your*).

You can express an opinion even if you don't say *I*. Your point of view is expected to be part of your writing. Most good writing would fall flat if it weren't for self-righteous opinions. Write as if your ideas and prescriptions were universal truths.

If you are trying to convince your readers of something, they will believe you if you are perceived to be an observer. No one thinks of a participant as having an open mind. Write 99 percent of your work in the second and third person, and reserve the first person for brief anecdotes and examples that draw on your experience. Once you've used the first person in an anecdote, however, be sure to return to the third person when the anecdote has ended.

THE DEGENDERIZATION OF LANGUAGE

This is a fancy way of saying there are ways to avoid sounding sexist. As you raise your consciousness, you become more aware of awkward linguistic problems.

The most common sexist tradition in the English language is the third-person singular pronoun, *he*, as in, "Anyone who says he doesn't like chocolate is crazy." This problem arises often and should be dealt with consistently. There are many options from which to choose:

• In the preface to your book, acknowledge the language problem and say, "Due to the lack of a better word, I will use *he* [or *she*] by default." See the Preface of this book for a case in point.

• Alternately use *he* and *she*, although this can become awkward and confusing.

• Use the plural *they* as in, "Writers who say they never confront this problem are either lying or writing in the first person." This is a workable solution, though it doesn't lend itself to much variety. It can also be misleading, as in, "Writers should clean their typewriters often." This awkward construction could be construed as meaning writers have more than one typewriter.

• Use the second person. Address your readers directly. The *you* is understood. This works well as long as it is not overused and doesn't sound condescending.

• Avoid the issue altogether. Construct sentences like this: "Everyone can learn to write faster and more creatively." This alternative works but not well. It creates sentences that have an aloof feeling to them. You want to be more conversational.

• Combine all of the options. You may have noticed that this book uses a combination.

Some words can easily be neutered. *Fireman, chairman,* and *salesman* can become *firefighter, chairperson,* and *salesperson*. Words ending in "-er" can be left alone; *waiter, waitress, actor, actress,* and *writer* are fine as they are. Don't try to be politically correct with words like *lumberjack*. After all, what is a lumberjill?

Some words are the victims of stereotyping. For example, *doctor, nurse, lawyer, librarian,* and *teacher* may evoke images of either men or women. The best approach is to use the third-person plural, lest you get in trouble. If you continually say things like, "The doctor, with his demanding workload, cannot waste time," someone is going to be offended. You're better off saying, "Doctors, with *their* demanding workloads . . ."

The way you orchestrate your words will be instrumental in how successfully you entertain, educate, and motivate your reading audience. Everyone knows the difference between the style of a eulogy and the style of a motivational speech. Good writers change their style to match the demands of the piece they are writing. Right now your forte is more verbal than literary, so concern yourself with editing your work for brevity, clarity, and precision. Later, as you gain experience, you can experiment with style.

SMALL STEPS TO SUCCESS

Work to Be Done   **Deadline**

1. Reread and study this chapter.   _____
2. Edit an article you wrote.   _____
3. Start a file of creative phrases, metaphors, and   _____
   analogies that you like.
4. Read a book or article by someone whose   _____
   writing you admire. Analyze how the author
   wins you over.
5. Edit something you wrote with an eye toward   _____
   brevity, clarity, and precision.
6. Write a letter or article, and use sentences of   _____
   varying lengths and constructions.
7. Rewrite a brief article from the newspaper,   _____
   putting it in your own words.

Get Started on This List Today

15

TIPS FOR GREATER PRODUCTIVITY

Prolific professional writers develop ways to increase their productivity, save time and money, and avoid burnout. We have gathered a collection of "the best of the best" from a variety of successful writers. In every phase of writing, from outlining the first draft to accepting a Pulitzer Prize, the hints in this collection will help you advance to new levels of productivity. Continually refer back to these tips until they become habits.

Write Quickly and Nonjudgmentally

This is one of the most salient tips in this book, one worth repeating several times. When writing a first draft, separate your creative drive from your analytical nature. Write as quickly as possible, getting every thought on paper in a conversational tone. Tap into a stream of thoughts, and let them flow. Avoid the temptation to stop to correct anything, especially typos. There will be ample time later to edit and rewrite.

Establish Deadlines

Most writers will admit that a deadline and the promise of money are a writer's best friends. Both serve to spur you on and give you the feeling there is some short-term as well as long-term value to your work. Deadlines guarantee you will finish the job rather than procrastinate indefinitely. If you don't have a collaborator or an editor to impose deadlines, set them yourself.

Set a Daily Quota

A quota will serve as a mini-deadline, forcing you to produce something daily. If you wait for inspiration before sitting down to write, you'll spend most of your time standing. Creativity is 75 percent perspiration, 25 percent inspiration. The perspiration, however, gets the creative juices flowing. So force yourself to sit and write—even just a letter—until you pick up momentum.

Work in Small Increments

Many writers freeze when they have a large project because the prospect of writing 200 or more pages seems overwhelming. Remember to break up a project into small, easily manageable tasks. One way to do this is to set a deadline and divide the number of pages to be written by the number of days until the deadline. You'll be surprised how easy it will look. You may only have to write three or four pages per day. Small but steady progress will get your book completed on time.

Neil Simon employs this method of writing. He writes every weekday morning and plays tennis every afternoon. He consistently writes three pages per day, so at the end of a week he has completed fifteen pages. At the end of ten weeks, he has finished the first draft of a screenplay.

Write When You Are at Your Best

Some of us are morning people, and some are night owls. You know when you function best. Whenever it is, try to get most of your creative work done at that time. If you can, structure your time so you can work in long, uninterrupted blocks. Continuous bursts of enthusiasm and productivity are precious. Don't let them be compromised by telephone calls or other distractions.

Plan Ahead

The easiest way to sit down to write is to know exactly what you will be working on. Gather your notes, articles, and books on the subject. Create an outline, and know where you are going to begin and what you want to say before you sit down to write. Being organized will give you direction, which will help the words flow.

Make Use of Downtime

If you are familiar with time management principles, then you know how to use downtime, those unstructured minutes and hours when you can't accomplish any time-consuming projects but can read short articles or balance your checkbook. Sitting in a traffic jam is downtime; so is sitting in the psychologist's waiting room, especially if you're depressed.

There are ways to creatively do nothing. You can read, relax, meditate, visualize yourself as the superstar you want to be, read your affirmations, listen to self-improvement tapes, think about your book, and so on. Bring materials with you when you expect to be waiting somewhere. You'd be surprised how much can be done in five- and ten-minute time slots.

Take Notes Anywhere, Anytime

Inspiration is like the proverbial butterfly—elusive. To get the most out of your fertile mind, be prepared to write down what pops up—anywhere, anytime. Most writers always carry a pen and pad. A tape recorder works even better. Dictating is faster than writing and can be done while driving or in the dark.

Taking notes in the middle of the night is well worth the effort and agony of turning on a light. While you sleep, your mind is percolating and brewing brilliant ideas. These intuitive flashes could have a significant impact on your project and—you never know—your life. Jonas Salk, the genius who discovered the polio vaccine, gives his unconscious mind a great deal of credit: "It is always with excitement that I wake up in the morning wondering what my intuition will toss up to me, like gifts from the sea. I work with it, and rely upon it. It's my partner."

Have a Comfortable, Functional Place to Write

Most writers work best in a quiet setting free of distractions. The aesthetics of your work area are unimportant, as long as you have a good source of light and fresh air. If you are fortunate enough to look out over the ocean or into a thicket of trees, all the better, but don't gaze out at your view at the expense of your work.

The kitchen table is the worst place to write. If you have a family or live with others, they will undoubtedly disturb you while raiding the refrigerator. In addition, the kitchen table usually has to be cleared for meals. The next time you work on your book, it will take longer to get started because of the setup time. If you don't already have them, buy a desk, chair, lamp, file cabinet, and any other items so you can establish a permanent work space for yourself.

Hang pictures on the wall for inspiration, or have someone take a picture of you in a bookstore holding up a book as if it were yours. If you aspire to driving a Porsche, hang a picture of yourself in front of one. These photos will serve as visual affirmations and spur you on.

Play CEO and Become Inaccessible

Many a train of thought has been broken by the telephone. After you have written for a while, you will appreciate the value of starting a train of thought and riding it to the end. It's too easy to lose an inspiration by answering the telephone, so put on your answering machine when you write.

Set aside a time, preferably before or after business hours, when you will be unavailable. The more you do this, the greater your productivity will be.

Avoid Mini-Freezes

There is another blocking phenomenon to be aware of in addition to writer's block: mini-freezes, unpredictable dry periods that occur while you are writing or before you begin. Some of the methods for avoiding mini-freezes have been passed down from generation to generation.

Stop when you're hot. Hemingway used this strategy. He would end his day's writing by leaving his work unfinished—actually stopping in the middle of a sentence. The next day he was forced to pick up where he left off. He preferred this to facing a blank page. Try it. Picking up your thoughts midstream may give you the instant momentum needed to jump right into your work.

Just as nature abhors vacuums, most writers hate a blank page. If a blank page freezes you, there is an easy way to defrost. Write in a stream of consciousness. Describe what you had for breakfast or the plot of the last movie you saw. Anything will do. Don't be critical. The objective is to prime the pump. Your writing will quickly become coherent, and a short way down the page you will find yourself back into writing your book. This concept ties in with the practice of nonjudgmental writing mentioned at the beginning of this chapter.

Kick the Avoidance Habit

Writers are notorious procrastinators. It is not uncommon to hear them trading stories of their rituals for delaying the moment of truth when they have to sit down, face the blank page, and be productive. Avoidance tactics run the gamut from compulsive pencil sharpening and calling friends to cleaning the entire house, including vacuuming the ceiling.

If you find yourself developing an avoidance ritual, recognize it for what it is—a writer's mini-block. Nip it in the bud. You'd be better off sitting down and writing gibberish than running around the house frantically looking for your muse. At least gibberish can be cleaned up and sold as a romance novel.

Work Anytime for Any Length of Time

There is a tendency to look at the clock and think, "I only have a half-hour; it's not worth getting started for so little time." Nonsense. Those little blocks of time add up like all the other small increments that comprise a book. The brilliant idea that popped up during a brief work session may never have appeared if you had waited for the perfect block of time.

Write in Your Head

When you are away from the computer, think about your material, and generate phrases, lead-in sentences, and other ideas. While driving, don't listen to the radio; think about your book. Often the most creative thoughts occur when the pressure is off, so take your tape recorder into the shower.

Before you go to bed at night and immediately upon rising, think about any problems you may be having with your project. Do what Jonas Salk does: Let your unconscious solve those problems.

Write Headlines to Sharpen Ideas

If you are writing an article or a book chapter, you can explore new angles by pretending you are writing a newspaper headline about your subject. Brainstorm ideas to see how they stimulate new ones.

Monitor Your Writing Habits

Imagine you are working two jobs: your day job where you have to spend forty hours a week and your writing job. In order to achieve your goal of writing articles or a book, you have to pay the dues, one of which is time. Finding the time is not a problem; the problem is consistently applying the seat of your pants to the seat of your chair.

Set aside the time to write, and then punch in as if you were going to another job. Do this by making a chart or using a calendar to record the number of hours spent writing each day. Punch in, and punch out. A glance at the chart after a week or two will be a shock. You may be surprised to find that being productive requires less time than you imagined.

On the other hand, you may find you have not been putting in enough time. Like many other writers, you may work like mad for a couple of days and let the memory of that hard work sustain you for a while. You walk around with a delusion of accomplishment. This self-deception could not possibly survive the punch card test.

Let the Words Age Before Editing

After writing a first draft, let it sit for at least a day or two before reading it again. This enables you to look at it more objectively (as if writers can ever look at their work objectively). The emotionally attached writer kicks and screams to prevent even one word being cut. The objective writer easily dons the critic's hat and calmly deletes the excess baggage as if the piece had been written by someone else. Yeah, sure.

Cut and Edit When You Are Tired

There will come a time at the end of your day when you are tired, there is nothing good on television, the kids are asleep, your spouse is out taking break-dancing lessons, and you want to get some work done despite the fog rolling across the bridge between your right brain and your left. Your choice is to try to muster the brain power to create something new or to edit a chapter or an article that is already written. The clear choice is to edit.

Being tired has its advantages. You will be less tolerant of wordiness and more inclined to cut superfluous words and sentences. In your cranky mood you will ask yourself, "What is the point? Why is this in here? How can I say this in fewer words?"—all excellent questions to ask yourself when editing.

Know Thyself

All the tips from the greatest writers in history are worthless if they don't ring true for you. The best advice is to discover what works best for you and then keep doing it.

Since self-exploration for exploitation is the best advice, all the Small Steps to Success, except for the first one, are optional. Aside from that one, if you think something will work for you, do it and monitor the results. If a suggestion rubs you the wrong way, ignore it. The item, however, should be practiced at least several times each week.

SMALL STEPS TO SUCCESS

Work to Be Done   **Deadline**

1. Write at least one page on anything, as long   _____
   as you write QUICKLY and NONJUDGMENTALLY.
2. Set a daily quota.   _____
3. Stop writing for the day in the middle of a   _____
   sentence or paragraph.
4. Arrange or rearrange your workplace for max-   _____
   imum comfort and convenience.
5. If you do not have one, create an office in   _____
   your home.
6. Write headlines for new angles.   _____

Get Started on This List Today

16

DICTATING CHAPTERS, TRANSCRIBING SPEECHES

People speak faster than they write, so why write when you can dictate? Unfortunately dictation is not a skill that comes easily to everyone. Anxiety about dictation machines is one of those irrational fears some people have, like fear of heights, snakes, or speaking in front of groups of people.

Dictation can be used to write first drafts, brainstorm ideas, and streamline correspondence time. The time needed to write things down physically is eliminated, so your thoughts flow quickly and easily, with fewer distractions. All this happens once you have become comfortable with the process.

The two primary fears concerning dictation are the fear of going blank and the fear of being grossly unorganized. Both are curable.

CURING DICTATION PHOBIA

Practice Daily

Your dictation will flow more quickly and smoothly when you relax. Relaxation will increase as you become more comfortable with the process. It is important to practice dictation, preferably 15 minutes or more each day.

When you practice, relax by telling yourself you are only practicing. The quality of the dictation is then unimportant. At first, don't even bother to rewind and listen to the tape. Simply concentrate on dictating in a comfortable, relaxed way. The important thing is to spend the time with your tape recorder so the two of you can learn to trust one another.

To become accustomed to dictating, begin by reading aloud something written by someone else. Choose a subject on which you are well versed because at some point you will put the book down and continue speaking on the subject. Give your opinion, add information, or simply speak your thoughts. Don't push yourself, and don't worry about continuity and organization. Simply pretend you are speaking to a friend on the telephone or in person. Use the pause button on the tape recorder when you want to stop to think. If you lose your train of thought, don't lose your cool; berating yourself will only slow your progress. Calmly collect your thoughts and continue. Make it fun, not a chore.

Think in Pictures

The easiest ideas to convey verbally are those you can visualize. This is true for dictation, speaking, and writing. An artist paints what he sees in his mind. When practicing dictation, describe scenes, people, your office, a movie, or anything else that will reinforce the connection between your visualizing right brain and your verbalizing left brain.

Speak Conversationally

Learning to dictate is similar to learning to write. At first, concentrate on getting your thoughts out as quickly as possible. This will help the flow and make you more productive. Dictate your ideas in simple English, and never pause to search for the perfect word. It's not worth the time and distraction. To mark the spot where you will later fill in the correct word, say something like "insert word here" or "find a better word for . . ." You can also say, "tk," if your transcriber will understand the term.

Try to keep your pace steady, but if you must pause, do so. When people learn to type faster, they sacrifice accuracy for speed. As they improve, accuracy and speed increase. Dictation is the same way. Don't worry about making too much sense in the beginning. Think far enough ahead to keep your sentences flowing.

Now that you know how to practice dictating, you are ready to learn the skills that will make serious composing much easier.

Outlines Are Essential

Good organization is the cornerstone of good writing and good dictation. The best way to overcome your phobia of going blank is to have the same detailed road map you have when writing—an outline. The same principles apply to dictating as to writing, so review the discussion of outlining techniques if necessary.

One additional step may help you dictate more smoothly: Turn each idea in your outline into a question. Some people find it easier to answer a question than to generate a discussion of a concept. For each question, give an answer that includes at least three supporting statements—statistics, anecdotes, abstract concepts, examples, or facts. The order is unimportant; you can always cut and paste later. Use the tricks that work best for you.

Your outline should be structured logically. For this reason, vertical outlines work best. Glance at your outline only when necessary; don't be distracted by it. Some people prefer to use index cards.

Make Life Easy for Your Transcriber

Whether your dictation will be transcribed by a full-time secretary or a spouse you have pressed into service, you will reduce their frustration by planning ahead. In addition, the first draft of your piece will read better if you heed the following suggestions:

Dictate in order of importance. Talking about the most important points first will obviate the need for extensive cutting and pasting later. The person transcribing the tape will be less frustrated if the order of your ideas is logical. If you are paying a secretary by the hour to transcribe your tape, you will spend less money if you are organized.

Log in before dictating. At the beginning of a session, state your name, the date, and the time. This is especially important if you are farming out your work to a busy word processing office. Another situation in which you need to identify yourself is in a collaboration. If both you and your partner are dictating chapters, it will be helpful later to know who wrote what. It is also a nice touch to start a tape with a friendly greeting to the transcriber, by name if you know it.

Give specific instructions. To insert an instruction, pause, change your tone, address the transcriber, and give the message. Be sure to make it obvious you are interrupting the flow of the text for an instruction. You can say, "Stop. Here is an instruction . . ." or "Stop, Shirley; at this point I'd like you to insert illustration 3 . . ."

If you are dictating a letter, specify details, such as the number of copies, to whom it will be sent and when the letters should be mailed. Be sure to tell your transcriber which draft of the transcript you want to see. When you read a transcribed article or book chapter, you don't mind seeing typographical errors. These will be fixed when you edit and rewrite. If you are dictating a business letter, however, the transcribed copy that you proofread had better be perfect. Inform your secretary of your expectations in advance.

Speak clearly. Enunciate. Hold the microphone about six inches from your lips, and speak over rather than directly into it. Record a sentence or two, and then play it back to see if the volume is correct. These technical details will soon become second nature.

Spell words when necessary. When dictating names, addresses, uncommon words, or words that can be spelled several ways, be on the safe side and spell them—slowly. If you don't know the proper spelling, make a note for the transcriber to look it up. When you give an abbreviation, make it clear that it is such, and spell it.

When spelling words, be aware that some letters sound like others. For example, B, C, D, E, G, P, T, V, and Z sound similar, especially on an unclear recording. One way to make yourself clear is to say things like, "B as in backgammon" and "T as in Tom." "If you want to be a perfectionist and show off, use the phonetic alphabet: Alpha, Bravo, Charlie, Delta, Echo, Foxtrot, Golf, Hotel, India, Juliette, Kilo, Lima, Mike, November, Oscar, Papa, Quebec, Sierra, Tango, Uniform, Victor, Whiskey, X-ray, Yankee, Zulu. Notice that none of these words has a homonym or rhymes with another word. Can you think of a word that sounds like Quebec or Oscar?

Spelling words and identifying the letters with the phonetic alphabet may seem a little farfetched, but these techniques come in handy when you dictate in a noisy airplane. If your tape has a constant noise in the background, your transcriber will appreciate the time you took to make yourself understood.

Punctuate if necessary. Depending on the ability of your transcriber and the nature of your text, you may have to punctuate as you dictate. Certainly it would be a nuisance to say "period" at the end of each sentence or "comma" at the end of each dependent clause, but there are times when you must (e.g., business letters that will not be edited and retyped). If you are working on an article or book, you can skip most of the punctuation, and add it during editing.

Some punctuation will be necessary, no matter what you are working on. Specify unusual formats such as lists, columns, quotation marks, underlined words, italicized words, question marks, parentheses, colons, semicolons, hyphens, dollar signs, exclamation marks, dashes, and so on. Insert your instructions by saying things like:

- "At the end of the consultation, the CEO stood up, shook my hand and said, [*change voice*] BEGIN QUOTE: 'Barbara, that was the most impressive analysis of our sales team I have ever heard. I am going to give you twice your regular consultation fee. [*change voice*] END QUOTE. And then I woke up."

- "PLEASE INDENT TEN SPACES AND LIST THE FOLLOWING WORDS."

- "To avoid confusing the operator [*change voice*] COMMA, and incurring an unnecessarily, UNDERLINE UNNECESSARILY, high transcribing expense COMMA, the speaker avoided stream HYPHEN of HYPHEN consciousness digressions PERIOD."

- "He used a lot of quotes and statistics and always ended his articles with the punch of a hard fact PERIOD. NEW PARAGRAPH."

Sign off at the end. Instead of stopping at the end of the last sentence, sign off with whatever comment you think is appropriate. This will prevent your transcriber from wondering what is next. You might also add a little pleasantry such as, "Thanks for your patience, Deb; the check is in the mail."

TRANSCRIBING SPEECHES

Many professional speakers write with their mouths, as it were. They have the advantage of being able to give a speech or training session, record it, and turn it into an article or part of a book chapter. The steps are similar to dictating, with the major exception being the setting and the intention of the recording.

Turning a speech into the first draft of an article or book chapter is a great way to start writing. This does not mean the work ends after leaving the podium. On the contrary, the majority of the work begins after the first draft is on tape. The following steps are an overview of the process of turning a speech into an article or book chapter. The details and fine points of each step are covered in the appropriate chapters in this book:

1. Have the tape transcribed and typed in double- or triple-space format. The extra space between lines will allow room for editing.

2. Read and edit the first draft as you would something that was composed on a computer.

3. When rewriting, pay attention to the content of the piece. Typically you will have to add a lot of information and delete a lot of filler to make it a marketable article. Speakers can get away with more anecdotes, jokes, and digressions than they can in print or on audio or video. To fill in the details and round out the chapter or article, add facts, statistics, historical background, and whatever else seems appropriate to the subject.

4. Analyze the style of the first draft. Speeches are often given in the first person; articles and book chapters are never written in the first person. Speeches are also much more conversational than articles. You may have to rewrite a great deal of the first draft to make it sound journalistically professional. Consult the editing and style chapters of this book for guidance.

GUIDANCE ON HARDWARE

You don't have to spend a fortune on dictation and transcribing equipment. The higher the quality of your equipment, however, the more conveniences you will have for yourself and your transcriber. If you are giving your tapes to an outside transcriber, you'll be saved the expense of the transcribing machine, which is the most expensive part.

Tape recorders vary in size from huge stereo portables to micro-cassette recorders that fit in a shirt pocket. Each has advantages and disadvantages.

A large, portable sound system is clearly overkill for dictating, but don't overlook one in a pinch. If a terrific idea comes to mind and you are caught without your usual recorder, you may be able to borrow one of these from someone nearby. Stranger things have happened on busy city street corners.

The largest tape recorder you should consider buying is the small desk types that measure approximately six by ten inches. These are portable and light enough to fit in a briefcase and run on batteries or can be plugged into a wall socket through an AC adapter. These models usually accept a combination microphone/on-off switch, a worthwhile option.

There are many advantages to these tape recorders. First, they use standard cassettes, so you can listen to self-help tapes, speeches, music, and other programs. Standard tapes give better fidelity than miniature tapes. You can record and listen to music and be reason-ably pleased with the sound quality.

The second advantage is durability. The larger the tape recorder is, the less fragile it will be. Because the mechanical and electronic parts are bigger and more rugged, you can abuse it with little guilt. When it does break, it will cost less to fix than a microcassette recorder. The only disadvantage is size. There may be times when you want a smaller tape recorder.

If you prefer the convenience of miniaturization or the high-tech James Bond look, consider buying a microcassette recorder. Some of these units are slightly larger than the palm of your hand and fit easily in a shirt or jacket pocket. They are great for dictating at a moment's notice. Microcassette recorders use miniature cas-settes that measure one and a quarter inches by two inches. All microcassette recorders run on batteries, and most accept power from optional AC adapters. Always carry a spare set of batteries. The sound quality is satisfactory for voice but unsatisfactory for music. Most microcassette recorders won't accept external microphones. The major advantage to microcassette recorders is their small size.

There are two major disadvantages to microcassette recorders:

They are more fragile and expensive to repair than larger models—in fact, it could cost more to repair one than to replace it—and they are less reliable and will not withstand abuse as larger tape recorders do. Everything inside is small, light, and packed tightly together.

Transcribing a tape without a transcriber is an arduous task. It can be done but requires you alternately to type and turn the unit on and off by hand. If you are going to transcribe a lot of material, save yourself and your transcriber the time and frustration. Invest in a transcriber that has a foot pedal, a remote control for stopping, starting, fast forwarding, and rewinding the tape. These machines are made for both standard recorders and microcassettes. Some machines can even take both sizes. Most office supply stores carry models by Sanyo, Dictaphone, Lanier, Sony, Norelco, and others.

For people who cannot find the time to sit and write, dictation offers a viable alternative. The flexibility is a great asset. Like any other tool, dictation takes practice and patience to become natural and feel comfortable. It is, however, a valuable skill well worth developing.

SMALL STEPS TO SUCCESS

Work to Be Done   **Deadline**

1. Buy a tape recorder, and practice using it   _____
   every day.
2. Dictate a simple business letter. Then work   _____
   your way up to an article.
3. Record and transcribe one of your speeches   _____
   or a module of a training session.
4. Edit and rewrite the transcript of a recorded _____
   speech.
5. Outline and dictate an article.   _____

Get Started on This List Today

17

FUEL YOUR PASSION

By now, if you have diligently worked on the Steps to Success in each chapter, you will have increased your motivation, writing ability, and confidence. If you read the book without completing the exercises, we *implore* you to go back through the chapters and do them. Start with Chapter 2 and build your enthusiasm again.

In Chapter 2 we discussed a formula for growth:

$$\text{Insight } + \text{ risk } = \text{ Growth.}$$

A slight variation of this formula is apropos at this time:

$$\text{Knowledge } + \text{ courage } + \text{ practice } = \text{ Success.}$$

Knowledge gives you the information you need to do what you want to do. Courage is necessary to face the risks involved in every new endeavor. Practice hones your skills and increases your knowledge and courage. It's a cyclical process—one that grows on itself and makes the whole process easier with time.

Now that you have the knowledge, we encourage you to muster the courage to practice, practice, practice. Never remain satisfied with your writing ability or the quality of your work. Strive for constant improvement—even perfection—and you will craft articles and books that you will be proud of. Never say, "This is good enough" until you have reread and rewritten something so many times that you are tired of it. There are no shortcuts to true talent and quality work.

To continue gaining knowledge, we recommend you read other how-to books on writing. To continue to train your ear for language, read novels, poetry, magazines, and articles that are well written. Don't read the newspaper for inspiration; newspaper articles are informative but often poorly written. Instead, read authors known for their quality, not quantity.

A good writer is captivating, moves you emotionally, and paints vivid pictures for you. Good writing takes a nonvisual medium and makes it dance with images, which is similar to making water out of hydrogen and oxygen; it takes a lot of effort, and yet the final product seems so natural. In any endeavor, the greats make it look easy.

Many people say they would like to write a book. Many people have at least one good novel or nonfiction book in them. The difference between those who talk about writing a book and those who write a book begins with one simple variable—passion. Fuel yours.

PART FIVE

Make A Name
For Yourself

18

MARKETING SAVVY
THAT WORKS

Let's assume your book has been published. Now what? The simple answer is to use it to get as much exposure as possible. Regardless of how it was published, you will have to play an active role in promoting it. You'll want to appear on all the radio and television talk shows you can. If your topic is right, you *will* appear on all the talk shows, but the chances of that happening are slim. Most of us write business books that aren't very trendy, exciting, or otherwise appealing to talk show audiences. This is not to imply that you may not be the next Ken Blanchard or Tom Peters. Only time—and concerted promotion—will tell.

THE PUBLISHER'S ROLE

The more promise your book holds, the more money your publisher will invest in its promotion. A publisher weighs many variables: the earnings potential of your work, the trendiness of your subject, the number of copies *you* might sell, your track record, and your charisma and salability. Obviously a publisher would rather promote a Jackie Collins–type author than a crusty old troll.

Authors with past successes have more clout than first-timers. In fact, authors who have sold a lot of books can insert a clause into their contracts that stipulates a dollar amount to be spent on promotion.

There are a couple of ways to know if your publisher plans to promote your book. Ask your editor. You can judge by the size of the advance you were given. Logic dictates that the larger the advance was, the more the publisher must promote your book to recover the investment. If your advance is $5,000, you can assume your book is toward the bottom of the publisher's priority list. Plan to do all the promotion yourself. In fact, your book may sink or swim based on *your* efforts.

Typically publishers distribute your book to bookstores, offer it to relevant (trade-specific) book clubs, and try to arrange special sales. Special sales are large-quantity sales to corporations and professional associations—the same groups that you will target to promote your book.

SPECIAL SALES

To help your publisher market your book, do some homework even before you begin to outline Chapter 1. Target your market. Develop a list of professional and trade associations and corporations (present and former clients) that might be interested in quantity sales. For corporate clients, hazard a guess as to the number of books you might sell to them (perhaps one for each member of the sales force); for associations, write down the number of members. Present this "direct sales" list to your editor. If your publisher is reluctant to use this information to market your book aggressively, you can use the information for your own direct sales effort.

When we began writing this book, we drew up a list of associations to which it might appeal. There were more groups than we had imagined, ranging from Toastmasters International with 110,000 members to the Society of Professional Management Consultants with 160 members. Just from a cursory tally of professional associations, we saw a potential market of over 200,000 readers.

SPECIAL HOOKS

Your direct sales list will be composed of companies and associations linked to the industries that you address in your book. There's more, though. Find companies that are tangentially related to the book. Let's say you've written a book on customer service and have mentioned the Ritz-Carlton Hotel as a shining example. You now have a hook with which to approach the Ritz-Carlton to see if the hotel corporation will buy a large quantity of books to give away as gifts. Naturally your topic has to be inherently interesting to them. It's unlikely they would buy a book on the care and feeding of mulch bacteria just because their name was mentioned once.

Finding hooks does not mean you contrive hooks. Don't find excuses for mentioning company names just so you can approach them later for special sales. We don't plan to contact the Ritz-Carlton to buy this book (although it would be nice of them to give a copy to every consultant who passed through their doors).

Before you try to sell a company or professional association on the idea of buying a large quantity of books, talk to your publisher about customizing orders. It's possible that, for quantities of 500 or 1,000, you can have a company's logo and the CEO's testimonial printed on the book cover.

There is a way to customize books even more for special sales. Some books use in-depth examples or case studies to illustrate the principles being discussed. If your book is one of these, you can tell a company or professional association that you will tailor relevant discussions and insert industry- or company-specific examples into the book. Through computerization, the publishing business has become much more flexible, making extensive customization a viable marketing strategy.

THE BOOK-AS-BROCHURE

What would you rather have: (a) a $5,000 advance or (b) 1,000 free books? Think carefully before you answer. We hope you're *not* thinking: "1,000 books × $10 profit = $10,000. Hey, that's better than the $5,000 advance!" The right answer is *b* but not for that reason. Think of the big picture. Your advance copies would be used as highly effective brochures. Send them to prospective clients, and watch your calendar fill up. This is the instant credibility you have worked so diligently to achieve. Books are more than a product to sell; they are the most effective marketing tool you will ever have. Use them as such.

In the long run, your free books will bring in more money than a cash advance. Each consulting job or speech presents the opportunity to sell more books and gain exposure to more people; each person with a book is a prospective new client. You can see how your book-as-brochure will start a snowball effect. So don't be tightfisted; give those books away.

If you feel more comfortable looking at the short-term bottom line, consider this simple equation. You're given an advance of 1,000 books, all of which are sent out as promotional tools. If your closing ratio is 10:1, you will get 100 speeches, consulting jobs, or training sessions from the 1,000 books. If you get $2,000 for your services, you've grossed $20,000. That's still far better than the publisher's $5,000 advance or the $10,000 gross from selling those books.

There is another advantage to using your book as a promotional tool: Clients often call to discuss your area of expertise. Instead of taking the time on the telephone to explain every nuance of what you do, tell your prospective client that you will send a complimentary copy of your book. This accomplishes several purposes:

1. It saves time on the telephone—time that you can better use to gather information about your prospective client's needs.

2. It creates a powerful impression when your prospect receives the book.

3. It familiarizes your prospect with your material and gives him the opportunity to find something of interest—something you may not have mentioned in your telephone conversation.

4. It gives your prospect the ability to make specific requests for the content of your program.

Many consultants wonder why they should send books and risk giving away all their secrets. Why would a prospect bother to hire you after reading your book? This way of thinking is somewhat logical but not based in reality.

Let's face it. You go to the bookstore, and what do you find? *Innumerable* books on every conceivable subject, including your specialty. Yet there is still plenty of business for consultants, speakers, and trainers. Why aren't prospective clients just reading the books?

The bottom line is that people want the real thing, namely you. Sales managers know that books could never be a substitute for a live trainer. CEOs can't read about strategic planning and make changes the way they can with the guidance of a good consultant. Your book may clearly solve a major problem, but you will still be hired to tailor a presentation for the company or guide it through the change process step by step.

Another reason you shouldn't worry about giving away secrets is that people learn in different ways. Some things can be learned by reading, others only by doing. You can't learn to waterski by reading a book, but a book on waterskiing might get you motivated and provide enough theory to get you started. The same can be said of writing articles and books. This book motivated you to get started by providing some guidelines for making the task easier and less intimidating.

If you give keynote speeches, sending books will rarely hurt you; they can only help. There are no substitutes for keynote speeches. Can you imagine a convention in which, in lieu of the keynote speaker, they gave a book to everyone in the audience and announced that for the next hour everyone should read Chapters 8 through 11! The only place that would work is in a Woody Allen movie.

Writing articles and books—and producing audio and video tapes—does not close doors by satisfying needs. It creates opportunities by generating exposure and establishing your expertise.

BUYING BOOKS FROM THE PUBLISHER

Now that you realize how important your book-as-brochure is, try to negotiate the best deal with your publisher. Strive for the best discount on books that you will buy directly. What is a good deal? It has several aspects:

1. Ideally you do not have to order a minimum number of copies to get the best discount.
2. The books you buy are returnable.

3. The publisher will drop ship your orders (ship books directly to your customers and forward the bill to you).

A publisher who thinks of you as an author/entrepreneur—someone who will aggressively market books—will be more inclined to give you generous book club terms. First-time authors with the financial resources may have to guarantee the purchase of a large number of books (perhaps 1,000) in the first year. And for first-time authors, the publisher may stipulate that your books are nonreturnable. This reduces the publisher's bookkeeping costs.

When you are negotiating this aspect of your contract, assure your editor that you will not be competing with the publisher's efforts to sell books. Let your editor know that your books are intended for promotional use and direct sales to your clients.

CONTACTING CORPORATIONS AND ASSOCIATIONS

When you contact a company regarding group sales, seek out the director of training or the manager of a specific department. They have a constant need for new training materials, which they either make available to employees or give them outright.

The person to contact at a professional association is the director of education or of member services. One of the services that professional associations provide for their members is to find relevant educational materials and make them available at discount prices.

Most associations ask for a significant discount off the list price of your book—perhaps 50 percent. They then turn around and make a modest profit—what they call "nondues revenue." This source of income is very important to them. Here is an opportunity to make a quantity sale and customize the book cover for the group.

GET PUBLISHED IN ASSOCIATION NEWSLETTERS

Another way to gain exposure through professional associations is to write for their newsletters and magazines. Strike a deal: After getting your publisher's permission, offer to let the association adapt articles from your book for free in exchange for a plug (at least) at the end of the article that says, for example, "This article was adapted from *Publish and Flourish—A Consultant's Guide* by Garry

Schaeffer and Dr. Tony Alessandra (John Wiley & Sons, 1992). For more information on book sales and seminars, call 619-584-1846."

Ask for more. Offer to provide three articles based on your book in exchange for a half-page display ad. Your ad should appear in one of the issues in which your articles will be published. An ad that appears in the same issue as an article will have a tremendous impact.

THE DIRECT-MAIL OPTION

Every professional association has a computerized mailing list of its members. If you have the time, manpower, and money, you can buy some lists and send out a direct-mail letter accompanied by a professionally produced, one-page "brochure" on the book.* The one-page brochure should have a picture of the cover, a description, a list of the book's contents, some benefit statements, and testimonials from—hopefully—high-profile people.

Before you gear up to mail 100,000 letters, test the waters. Target your market carefully. Send out a test letter to 250 to 400 people—whatever you are financially comfortable with. Then sit back and wait for responses. If you get enough pull from your letter to make a profit, then you can justify a mailing of 1,000 pieces. If your campaign is a dud, you'll have lost only a reasonable amount of money.

PLAN YOUR FRONTAL ATTACK

The ideal way to penetrate an industry—to sell books, consulting services, speeches, or training—is to bombard it from all sides at once. Publish articles, place ads, send out direct-mail letters, and give speeches at local professional, trade, and corporate management meetings—even if you have to speak for free in the beginning. Your goal is to create name recognition, credibility, and word-of-mouth advertising. Then you can expect prospects to knock at your door or—better—call your 800 number.

---

*Mailing list brokers and other sources for names can be found in *Literary Market Place*, through professional and trade associations, and from other sources in Appendix C.

PRESS RELEASES

You have to be your own PR firm, which includes writing and sending press releases to local newspapers, professional journals, trade associations, and current and prospective clients.

Make your press release catchy and no longer than one page. Give a condensed version of the information in your brochure (if you have one). Don't overlook one of the most important bits of information: where the book can be purchased. If your publisher hasn't written a release you can use, you can probably request sample press releases from your publisher's publicity department or find inspiration in the sample in Figure 18.1.

Press releases serve two purposes. The more obvious is to announce your book's publication. Additionally, when a press release is sent to prospective clients, it serves to keep your name in front of them. As big advertisers know, every reminder counts and increases name recognition.

SPINNING OFF THE BOOK

You cannot write your book and expect miracles to happen. You've got to promote yourself with your new book, and you've got to sell books. Find out from your publisher how many units must be sold annually to keep your book in print. Make that number your annual sales quota.

There's more. Start thinking about ideas for spinoffs from the book. The more products you build around the original concept, the longer your book's life cycle will be. Think about producing an audiocassette program, either in association with your publisher and Nightingale-Conant or on your own. (Refer to your publishing contract for audio and video rights.) Videotape your speeches and workshops, and package them. Produce training videos in a studio. Hire a computer wizard to write a software program based on your specialty. Write a workbook—a greatly condensed form of your book—to accompany all of these new products. And when you promote them, devise ways to package them so the deal always includes the original book.

All of this is not new to you. You are aware of the range of products available from the top consultants, speakers, and trainers around the country. The key now is for you to develop a product line. It all starts with writing articles and then a book.

(619) 294-4388
(619) 294-4389

428 Thorn Street · San Diego, CA 92103

ADVERTISING   ·   MARKETING   ·   CREATIVE SERVICES

PUBLISH AND FLOURISH
A Consultant's Guide:
How To Boost Visibility and Earnings
Through a Publishing Strategy

PRESS RELEASE
FOR IMMEDIATE RELEASE

Savvy marketing advice for consultants, speakers, and trainers is served up by professional writer Garry Schaeffer and keynote speaker Dr. Tony Alessandra.

Publish and Flourish smoothes the way for all professionals to write and market books and articles as a means of promoting their businesses. To motivate even the most reluctant aspiring writers, the authors have distilled the writing process into clearly defined, easily manageable increments.

By clarifying and demystifying article and book writing and marketing, Publish and Flourish puts a powerful promotional tool in the hands of professionals whose careers are built on public perception.

Publish and Flourish is enhanced by worksheets, sprinkled with humor and written in a light, friendly tone. It will be published by John Wiley & Sons in August, 1992.

- END -

Figure 18.1

RADIO AND TELEVISION

Not every book, and not every author, is well suited for promotion on radio or television. If your book has best-seller potential and you have even a modicum of charisma, your publisher will make the arrangements for you to get radio and television exposure. If not, you can gain some publicity on your own.

Contact Bradley Communications at (215) 259-1070, which publishes the *Radio and TV Interview Report*, a monthly catalog of personalities and subjects that are available for interviews. You buy an ad and wait for radio stations to call. They will ask to interview you by telephone and set up a time to do so. You'll get to talk about your topic and plug the book.

There are advantages and disadvantages to using the *Interview Report*. On the negative side, you cannot target your audience. Your interview may be heard at 5:30 A.M. by Iowa farmers plowing their fields. The interviews may be logistically difficult to schedule if you are busy. The interviews could take thirty to forty-five minutes out of your day. Finally, it is difficult to sell books in this way; after all, relatively few commuters will write down the information needed to place an order.

On the positive side, the *Interview Report* is an efficient way to let a lot of radio stations know about you and your topic. You may find yourself invited to do a lot of interviews, which can be very flattering and fun, at least in the beginning. Finally, a lot of people may hear your name over the air, which is important if your primary goal is to increase your name recognition. And, you never know, the right person may hear you and call to hire you.

Most readers of this book are frequent travelers. Take advantage of your mobility by arranging interviews in the cities in which you will be working. You can have your office do the legwork of contacting radio stations and small, local television stations, or you can hire a PR firm to arrange the interviews. This is especially useful for people who conduct public seminars. Consultants who work behind closed doors with managers and executives will not be able to invite the public to see them, but the airtime will still serve to increase exposure.

If you plan to hire a PR firm to handle your interview schedule, try to find one that charges only for what it accomplishes. Instead of paying a monthly retainer, which every PR firm prefers, negotiate to pay one flat fee for radio interviews and another, higher fee for television interviews. Expect to pay more for both types of interviews in large markets.

If your book has a lot of potential, the publisher will take an active role in setting up media interviews and paying your expenses for a tour. If your book has moderate potential, your publisher may not offer much in the way of promotion, but everything is negotiable. You may be able to get your publisher to pick up half of the expenses of a tour to the top ten markets in the United States (or some other arrangement).

REVIEWS

Reviews are an effective form of publicity that you and your publisher should exploit. Depending on the nature of your book, your publisher may have a list of reviewers to whom they plan to send your book. Ask your editor if such a list exists for your book. If so, ask to see it. Add or substitute better (industry-specific) reviewers as you see fit.

If your publisher does not intend to send your book to reviewers, devise your own list of editors and book reviewers from professional and trade association newsletters, association executives, and other sources.

When you send your book to a reviewer, include a cover letter that describes it and its intended audience. This cover letter should be factual, not a PR piece. Leave the hyperbole to the reviewer.

TESTIMONIALS

One of the most important promotional tools that you will use is testimonials. Before your book is published or even accepted for publication, send copies of the manuscript to influential people who will write testimonials for you. These testimonials, aka blurbs, will appear on the front and back covers of the book and help your marketing efforts.

Two factors determine the salience of your testimonials: the stature of the person who wrote it and his relevance to your target market. Obviously a blurb will carry more weight if it comes from someone who is highly respected or admired and who people care about. A cover blurb by Michael Milken would be totally ineffective on a book about business ethics; it would be quite effective on a book about the inner workings of the junk bond market.

NOVELTY ITEMS

A book is a product. There is no reason why you should not be creative in the promotion of your product. Think of novelty items that can be imprinted with your name, the name of the book, and your toll-free telephone number. These novelties can be humorous, functional, or both. You may have seen the crooked pens that say, "I love my chiropractor."

Try to tie the novelty to your field. Financial planners can distribute abacuses; professional speakers can send a pound of tongue; and defense attorneys can send hacksaw blades.

Novelties that last and are useful will have a greater impact than ones that are perishable or consumable. Food, candy, and flowers are nice, but they disappear quickly—along with the reminder of you and your book. Send items that will be useful or valued for their entertainment value.

The key to promotion is positive exposure. Create a plan to gain as much exposure as you can through television and radio interviews, press releases and other publicity, direct mail, and other means that suit your profession.

SMALL STEPS TO SUCCESS

Work to Be Done   **Deadline**

1. List at least ten corporations or professional   _____
   associations to target for special sales of your
   book.
2. Identify the person to contact at the compa-   _____
   nies or associations listed in Step 1.

3. Make a list of conventions or trade shows at _____
   which you might set up a booth to sell your
   book and your services.

4. Draw up a list of at least five influential peo- _____
   ple to whom you can send your book for a
   testimonial.

5. Make a list of journal, magazine, or news- _____
   letter editors or reviewers to whom to send
   your book.

6. Write a one-page press release that has a _____
   strong, relevant angle to it (other than
   "here's a new book").

7. Make a thorough list of people to whom to _____
   send press releases.

8. Contact a professional writer and/or graphic _____
   artist about developing a new brochure for
   yourself and one for your book.

9. If you plan to self-publish, contact three to _____
   five book wholesalers to find out what they
   require to distribute your book.

10. Target a market for direct mail promotion, _____
    and find out the details of purchasing a mail-
    ing list.

11. Find a graphic artist to design an ad for your _____
    book.

12. Make a list of publications in which you will _____
    place ads.

13. Contact the publications listed in Step 12 _____
    regarding articles, trades for ads, and ad
    rates.

Get Started on This List Today

APPENDIX A

SOURCES OF INFORMATION

If you can't find the information you need from the following sources, it probably does not exist. Ask a librarian to familiarize you with the sources that are relevant to your field or your information search.

PUBLIC LIBRARY

Card catalog

Reader's Guide to Periodical Literature

Business Periodicals Index

Reader's Guide to Scientific Literature

Computerized indexes, such as INFOTRAC

Who's Who books

Corporate annual reports

Directories of associations (e.g., *Gale's Encyclopedia of Associations*, national trade and professional associations)

Directory of Directories

U.S. Manufacturers Directory

The magazine index

The newspaper index

Editorials on File

Facts on File

Major newspaper indexes: *Wall Street Journal, New York Times, Washington Post*

Magazine sources
  Working Press of the Nation
  Bacon's Publicity Checker
  Writer's Market
  Literary Market Place
  Standard Rate and Data Service

Miscellaneous reference books
  Blue Books, Red Books
  Thomas' Register
  Cahner's Buyer's Guide
  Directory of Conventions
  Current Baker Library Publications

Ulrich's International Guide to Periodicals

SPECIAL LIBRARIES

Graduate school libraries
  Business, Engineering, Medicine, Law
  Thesis and dissertation indexes

Federal depository libraries

Federal libraries

Library of Congress

Corporate libraries

FEDERAL GOVERNMENT

U.S. Statistical Abstract

Public Information Office

Freedom of Information Office

Commissioned reports

Publication Center, Pueblo, Colorado 81009

National Technical Information Service, 5285 Port Royal Road, Springfield, Virginia 22161

Government Printing Office

National Referral Center

Federal Register

Federal Executive Directory

Agency publications
    Internal Revenue Service
    Department of Commerce
    Securities and Exchange Commission
    Department of Labor
    Small Business Administration
    Department of Defense
    Bureau of the Census
    Abstracts, agency newsletters

Telephone hot-lines

CONGRESSIONAL

Congressional Record

Annual reports

Hearings, acts, summaries

Reports of subcommittees

Congressional Quarterly
    1414 22d St. NW, Washington, DC 20037

STATE

State agencies (e.g., departments of commerce, transportation, and energy; environmental protection agencies)

State capital, governor's office

State library

Senators' and representatives' offices

Statewide commissions

REGIONAL, CITY, AND TOWN

Chamber of commerce

Planning committees

Consumer relations

Town hall, courthouse

Newspapers, telephone company

Highway commission

Police and fire departments

INFORMATION COMPANIES

Gale Research Co.
835 Penobscot Building
Detroit, MI 48226

Public Affairs Information Service
11 West 40th Street
New York, NY 10018

McGraw-Hill
1221 Avenue of the Americas
New York, NY 10020

National Research Bureau
310 South Michigan Avenue, #1150
Chicago, IL 60604

Facts on File
460 Park Avenue
New York, NY 10016

John Wiley & Sons
605 Third Avenue
New York, NY 10158

Guide to DRI Data Bases
Data Resources, Inc.
1750 K Street, NW
Washington, DC 20006

Management Contents
P.O. Box 3014
Northbrook, IL 60062

Rodale Press
33 East Minor Street
Emmaus, PA 18049

Predicasts
11001 Cedar Avenue
Cleveland, OH 44106

Ruff Times-Target Pub.
P.O. Box 2000
San Ramon, CA 94583

AMACOM
135 West 50th Street
New York, NY 10020

Guide to American Directories
B. Klein & Sons
P.O. Box 8503
Coral Springs, FL 33065

PERSONAL COMPUTER DATABASE SERVICES

Compu Serve, Inc.
500 Arlington Central Boulevard
Columbus, OH 43220

The Source
1616 Anderson Road
McLean, VA 22107

Dialog
3460 Hillview Avenue
Palo Alto, CA 94304

Bibliographic Retrieval Service
1200 Route 7
Latham, NY 12110

Find/SVP
500 Fifth Avenue
New York, NY 10036

Special Libraries Association
235 Park Avenue
New York, NY 10003

Data Bases for Business
Chilton Book Company
Radnor, PA 19089

Federal Data Base Finder
Information USA
12400 Beall Mt. Road
Potomac, MD 20854

CREATIVE INFORMATION SOURCES

Ralph Nader–sponsored groups

Underground and alternative publications
    Alternative Press Directory
    Box 1347
    Ansonia Station, NY 10023

Common Cause, Greenpeace, Sierra Club, National Organization for
    Women

NEWSLETTERS

Newsletter Association of America
1341 G Street, #603,
Washington, DC 20005

Newsletter Clearinghouse
Box 311
Rhinebeck, NY 12572

Oxbridge Directory of Newsletters
183 Madison Avenue, Room 1108
New York, NY 10016

National Trade & Professional Association
Columbia Books
777 14th Street
Washington, DC 20005

APPENDIX B

SAMPLE COLLABORATION AGREEMENT

This collaboration agreement illustrates the range of issues that can arise when taking on one or more partners.

This agreement between Frank J. Tortollini, residing at 7161 Lasagna Street, Gourmet, CA 92037 (herein called FRANK) and Woody Simon, residing at 4544 Smart Alek Ave. #10, Talent, CA 92116 (herein called WOODY) and Marvin S. Kreplach, residing at 7975 Bagel 'N Lox Blvd., Sesame, CA 92123 (herein called MARVIN).

WITNESSETH:

The parties desire to collaborate in the writing of a book, on the terms hereinafter set forth.

Now Therefore, in consideration of the promises, and of the mutual undertakings herein contained, and for other good and valuable consideration, the parties agree as follows:

1. The parties hereby undertake to collaborate in the writing of a certain non-fiction book (herein called The Book), dealing with business as it applies to Zen, and provisionally entitled *What You Don't See, You Don't Get.*

2. It is the intention of the parties that the completion of the book will meet the following conditions:

a) FRANK and MARVIN will be responsible for the conceptualization of the contents of the book. MARVIN will have the primary responsibility for conducting all interviews required for The Book.

b) FRANK will have the responsibility of selling the book to a publisher or finding a literary agent to represent the book.

c) WOODY will participate in the conceptualization, contact interviewees, and will have the sole responsibility of writing and editing The Book.

d) FRANK will have the right of final approval of all contents of The Book provided he shall use reasonable judgment in his final determination.

3. The parties contemplate that they will complete the manuscript of The Book by September 1, 19xx. If they fail to do so, they may by mutual written agreement extend the time for completion. In the absence of any such extension, they shall endeavor to fix by negotiation their respective rights in the material theretofore gathered and written, and in the project itself, i.e., whether one or the other of them shall have the right to complete The Book alone or in collaboration with someone else, and on what terms. Their understanding as to these matters shall thereupon be embodied in a settlement agreement. If they are unable to agree, their respective rights and the terms pertaining thereto shall be fixed by binding arbitration. In either event, this agreement shall cease when the rights of the parties have been fixed as aforesaid; and thereafter they shall have only such rights and obligations as will be set forth in the settlement agreement or the arbitration award, as the case may be.

4. Each party shall have the right to make contacts for the sale to a publisher or representation of The Book, but they shall keep each other fully informed with reference thereto and any agreement for the sale or representation shall require the consent of at least one other party. All parties agree that FRANK will have the exclusive right to negotiate the final agreement for the disposition of The Book or any of the subsidiary rights.

5. The copyright in The Book shall be obtained in the names of all parties and shall be held jointly by them.

6. The parties shall receive equal authorship credit in type of equal size, in alphabetical order by last name. Therefore, the order of the names will be: Kreplach, Simon & Tortollini. Any variation of this provision is subject to written approval of all parties.

7a. All receipts and returns from the publication of The Book and from the disposition of any subsidiary rights therein shall be divided as follows: 50% for WOODY, 25% for FRANK, and 25% for MARVIN, regardless of the means of promotion, distribution and sales. (See exception under clause 7b.) All agreements for publication and for the sale of subsidiary rights shall provide that each party's share shall be paid directly to him.

b) All parties agree that the publisher's advance will be divided differently from all subsequent receipts from The Book and any subsidiary rights. The publisher's advance will be divided in the following manner:

i) The literary agent's commission, if any, will be deducted first. A sum of $6,000 will be deducted next and paid to WOODY. Next, expenses totaling $10,000 or less which have been incurred by FRANK and MARVIN will be deducted and paid to FRANK and/or MARVIN. The remaining advance will be divided as follows: 50% for WOODY, 25% for FRANK and 25% for MARVIN.

ii) It is agreed that any publisher's stipend for typing, editing or any other manuscript preparation services will be paid to WOODY and that he will take responsibility for providing these services. This stipend in no way affects the conditions of clause 7a or 7ai.

c) It is agreed that all expenses incurred in the research, travel, interviews, preparation and writing of The Book will be incurred by FRANK and MARVIN. Total reimbursement will not exceed $10,000 and will follow the procedure outlined in clause 7bi.

8. The rights for the development of subsequent projects based on the theme or content of The Book shall be held by each party as follows:

All Audio/Video/Electronic Rights .... FRANK
Serialization Rights .... See clause 8c
Novelty Rights (e.g., t-shirts, etc.) .... WOODY
Related Books .... ALL THREE

a) In the development of future projects based on the theme or content of The Book for which the parties hold the rights, no party may collaborate with an outside party without first giving the parties in this agreement the first right of refusal to participate in the project. Royalty shares for future projects involving the parties will be negotiable; however, the originator, developer, or holder of the rights of the project will receive at least 50%.

b) In the event of the death of one or more of the authors, all present and future rights held by that person will be transferred to the surviving author(s).

c) Serialization rights, that is, condensations and excerpts of the book appearing before the publication of the book and negotiated by the publisher or the authors' agent, shall be construed as part of The Book. The rights and receipts thereof shall be divided in accordance with clause 7a.

d) Each party has the right to sell magazine and journal articles based on the book and to keep 100% of the receipts from said pieces. Such serializations will only be undertaken after the publication of The Book and will adhere to the following conditions:

i) Each party has the right to claim first authorship of said articles but must give second and third authorship in alphabetical order and in the same type size to the other parties.

ii) In publications that allow an author's biography, the first author of the article will include the biographies of the other parties, if possible.

9. The personal promotion of The Book shall meet the following conditions:

a) When possible, all three authors will appear together to promote The Book. This includes but is not restricted to all forms of promotion such as TV, radio, print media, and personal appearances. All parties will make every reasonable effort to include the others in promotional opportunities.

b) If it is possible for only one author to make a promotional appearance, all parties agree that it will be FRANK. If FRANK is unable to appear, MARVIN will appear, except six months after the publication of the book, clause 9c will take effect.

c) If, six months after the publication of the book, the authors are not satisfied with the promotional efforts of the publisher, it is agreed that a Public Relations firm will be hired to handle the authors' promotional appearances. The costs for the P.R. firm will be split equally among the authors and appearances will be determined by a rotation system, the order of which will be FRANK, MARVIN, and WOODY.

d) Any compensation for promotional appearances will be divided equally among the three parties, regardless of who made the appearance, with deductions for expenses being taken off the top, if necessary.

10. Speaking engagements on the theme or content of The Book will meet the following conditions:

a) Each party is entitled to promote himself for speaking engagements not intended solely for book promotion but covering the theme or content of The Book. No party has the right to a share of receipts from the others' speaking engagements.

b) In all written promotional material, each party must represent himself as the co-author of The Book.

c) Professional speaking on the theme of The Book shall take place only after a contract has been signed with a publisher. The only exception to this is for WOODY to make free local speeches on the subject.

d) Each author agrees to give the other parties the first right of refusal on all speaking engagements not personally accepted by him. A commission of 20% will be due to the referring party by the party accepting the engagement.

11. If the parties by mutual agreement select an agent to handle the publication rights of The Book or the disposition of the subsidiary rights therein, and if the agent is authorized to make collection for the parties' account, such agent shall remit each party's share direcly to him in accordance with clauses 7a and 7bi.

12. After the completion of the manuscript of The Book, no change or alteration shall be made therein by any party without the others' consent. However, such consent shall not be unreasonably withheld. No consent to make a specific revision shall be deemed permission for an overall revision.

13. No author may transfer anything except royalties to another party other than one of the other authors. If an author (herein called the First Party) desires to transfer his share in The Book's royalties to another person, he shall give written notice by registered mail to the other authors (herein called the Other Parties) of his intention to do so. Said notice will be delivered to the addresses in the preamble of this agreement or to another address provided from time to time by each to the others in writing.

a) In such case the Other Parties shall have an option period of 30 days to purchase the First Party's share at a price and upon such terms indicated in the written notice, which price and terms shall be at least as favorable as those offered to any non-party to this agreement.

b) If the Other Parties fail to exercise their options in writing within the aforesaid period of 30 days, or if, having exercised it, they fail to complete the purchase upon the terms stated in the notice, the First Party may transfer his rights to another person on terms no more favorable than those stated in the notice; and he shall forthwith send to the Other Parties a copy of the contract of sale of such rights, with a statement that the transfer has been made.

c) If the First Party fails for any reason to make such a transfer to another party, and if he desires to make a subsequent transfer to someone else, the Other Parties' option shall apply anew to such proposed subsequent transfer.

14. Nothing herein contained shall be construed to create a partnership between the parties. Their relation shall be one of collaboration on a single work, with subsequent works to be negotiated separately.

15. If The Book is published, this agreement shall continue for the life of the copyright therein. Otherwise the duration hereof shall be governed by the provisions of clause 3.

16. If any party dies before or after the completion of the manuscript, the surviving parties to this agreement shall have the right to complete The Book, to make changes in the text previously prepared, to negotiate and contract for publication and for the disposition of any subsidiary rights, and generally to act with regard thereto as though they were the sole

authors, except that (a) the name of the decedent shall always appear as a co-author; and (b) the survivors shall cause the decedent's share of the proceeds to be paid to his estate, and shall furnish to the estate true copies of all contracts made by the surviving parties to this agreement pertaining to The Book.

17. Any controversy or claim arising out of or relating to this agreement or any breach thereof shall be settled by arbitration in accordance with the Rules of American Arbitration Association; and judgment upon the award rendered by the arbitrators may be entered in any court having jurisdiction thereof. If the parties are unable to agree on an arbitrator, each shall choose an arbitrator, and lots shall be drawn for the final selection. The terms of this contract shall be construed and interpreted pursuant to the laws of the State of California.

18. This agreement shall inure to the benefit of and shall be binding upon the executors, administrators, and assigns of the parties.

19. This agreement constitutes the entire understanding of the parties, and no modification shall be valid unless it is in writing and signed by the parties to be bound.

IN WITNESS WHEREOF the parties hereunto set their respective hand and seal this _____ day of _____, 19xx.

_____
Frank J. Tortollini

_____
Woody Simon

_____
Marvin S. Kreplach

WITNESSES:

_____

_____

Date: _____   Date: _____

APPENDIX C

SELF-PUBLISHING AND MARKETING RESOURCES

No book can be all things to all readers. This appendix will guide you to other sources to help you with your motivation, writing, editing, self-publishing, and marketing. The resources available to you just in terms of books is astounding. If you add people as a resource, then there is an unbelievable amount of information out there waiting to be tapped.

Use the following books to get started and refer to their bibliographies for yet more books. When contacting any of the following organizations, find out if they have a toll-free telephone number.

THE BUSINESS OF SELF-PUBLISHING

American Book Trade Directory
R. R. Bowker
245 West 17th Street
New York, NY 10011
A directory of over 20,000 book outlets, wholesalers, and distributors in the United States and Canada. Entries are listed alphabetically by city and state.

American Library Directory
R. R. Bowker
245 West 17th Street
New York, NY 10011
A directory of libraries in the United States.

Bookmaking: The Illustrated Guide to Design, Production and Editing, by
          Marshall Lee
R. R. Bowker
245 West 17th Street
New York, NY 10011
A comprehensive book that covers the details of production and is especially valuable for those who will be taking an active role in the self-publishing process.

Business and Legal Forms for Authors and Self-Publishers, by Tad Crawford
Allworth Press
10 East 23d Street
New York, NY 10010
Send for a catalog of Allworth's other useful writing tools.

CSG Information Services
425 Park Avenue
New York, NY 10022
CSG (Chain Store Guide) directories help you find wholesalers and retailers serving your target market.

*The Writer's Lawyer: Essential Legal Advice for Writers and Editors in All
          Media*, by Ronald L. Goldfarb and Gail E. Ross
Times Books
201 East 50th Street
New York, NY 10022

Literary Market Place
R. R. Bowker
245 West 17th Street
New York, NY 10011
Find a library that has it, and familiarize yourself with this bible of the industry.

The Self-Publishing Manual, by Dan Poynter (Para Publishing, 1991)
A comprehensive guide to self-publishing.

MARKETING AND PROMOTION

Bacon's Publicity Checker
Bacon's
332 South Michigan Avenue
Chicago, IL 60604
This directory lists newspapers and magazines across the United States. Consult it to compile a list of editors to contact about articles and/or book reviews. Bacon's also sells mailing lists and provides a clipping service.

Book Publishing Resource Guide, by John Kremer
Ad-Lib Publications
51 North Fifth Street
Fairfield, IA 52556-1102
This directory lists book wholesalers, distributors, sales representatives, bookstore chains, book clubs, catalogs, marketing services, mailing list brokers, and more.

CMG Mailing List Catalog
CMG Information Services
50 Cross Street
Winchester, MA 01890
CMG offers a free directory of its mailing lists targeted to university professors, "decision-maker library lists," and others who buy books in a variety of topics.

Encyclopedia of Associations
Gale Research Co.
835 Penobscot Building
Detroit, MI 48226
This directory lists professional and trade associations by industry group. Available in most large libraries, this volume is an invaluable resource for marketing books.

Gale Directory of Publications and Broadcast Media, edited by Donald P.
          Boyden and John Krol
Gale Research Co.
835 Penobscot Building
Detroit, MI 48226
This directory, arranged geographically, is indexed alphabetically and by keywords. Use this directory when you are trying to gain media coverage.
      Also from Gale Research:
  Training and Development Organizations Directory
  Consultants and Consulting Organizations Directory

Information Industry Directory
Government Research Directory
Research Centers Directory

The Greatest Direct Mail Sales Letters of All Time, by Richard S. Hodgson
Dartnell Corp.
4660 Ravenswood Avenue
Chicago, IL 60640
Learn by example. This book shows what the best direct-mail copywriters
have written in a variety of marketing situations.

Guide to American Directories
B. Klein Publications, Inc.
P.O. Box 8503
Coral Springs, FL 33065
Another source for mailing lists of national organizations.

Hudson's Subscription Newsletter Directory
Hudson's
44 West Market Street
Rhinebeck, NY 12572
Provides information on newsletters around the world.

International Directory of Little Magazines and Small Presses
Dustbooks
P.O. Box 100
Paradise, CA 95967
Lists thousands of publications and publishing firms that may be interested
in articles.

National Radio Publicity Outlets
TV and Cable Publicity Outlets
Morgan Rand Publishing Co.
2200 Sansom Street
Philadelphia, PA 19103
These directories list thousands of radio and television programs, and their
contacts, topics, and formats.

National Trade and Professional Associations of the United States
Columbus Books, Inc.
1212 New York Avenue, N.W.
Washington, DC 20005
Lists over 6,300 organizations by industry, products, and geographical
location.

1001 Ways to Market Your Books for Authors and Publishers, by John
        Kremer
Ad-Lib Publications
51 North Fifth Street
Fairfield, IA 52556-1102

Professional's Guide to Public Relations Services, by Richard Weiner
AMACOM
135 West 50th Street
New York, NY 10020
Lists communication and image consultants, media directories, and other
publicity resources.

*Publicity for Books and Authors: A Do-It-Yourself Handbook for Small
        Publishing Firms and Enterprising Authors*, by Peggy Glenn
Aames-Allen Publishing Co.
1106 Main Street
Huntington Beach, CA 92648

Publisher's Weekly
249 West 17th Street
New York, NY 10011
A weekly trade newspaper that provides up-to-the-minute information
about book publishers, trends, and promotional opportunities. Find it in
your local library or subscribe.

Standard Periodical Directory
Oxbridge Communications, Inc.
150 Fifth Avenue, Room 636
New York, NY 10011
Data on more than 75,000 publications in the United States and Canada.

Standard Rate and Data Service
800-323-4588
Not unlike the *Standard Periodical Directory*, the SRDS provides information
on placing ads in newspapers and magazines.

Syndicated Columnists, by Richard Weiner
Larimi Communications
1515 Broadway
New York, NY 10036
Lists columnists who may want to review your book.

Thomas Register of American Manufacturers
Thomas Publishing Co.
One Penn Plaza
New York, NY 10119
One of a number of publications that can help you find companies to target for special sales.

Ulrich's International Periodicals Directory
R. R. Bowker
245 West 17th Street
New York, NY 10011
Lists more than 70,000 publications worldwide.

WRITING AND RESEARCH

The Authors Guild
330 West 42d Street
New York, NY 10036
A professional association that represents writers and literary agents in Congress and in the courts. A great deal of information can be gleaned from the monthly newsletter.

Directory of Special Libraries and Information Centers, edited by Brigette T.
        Darnay
Gale Research Co.
835 Penobscot Building
Detroit, MI 48226
Lists information centers, archives, and special libraries across the United States and Canada.

A **synonym finder** or **thesaurus**, in book and computerized forms

A **thesaurus** of **quotations**

A book of **anecdotes**

The Elements of Style, by William Strunk, Jr., and E. B. White
Macmillan
866 Third Avenue
New York, NY 10022

BOOKING CONTACTS AT TOP NATIONAL TELEVISION PROGRAMS

Maria Kell Brown, Producer
Arsenio Hall Show
Paramount Television
5555 Melrose Avenue
Swanson Building
Los Angeles, CA 90038
(213) 956-8500

Jay Kernis, Senior Producer
CBS This Morning
CBS-TV
524 West 57th Street
New York, NY 10019
(212) 975-2824

Jose Pretlow, Producer
Donahue
30 Rockefeller Plaza
New York, NY 10112
(212) 664-6501

Story Ideas
Geraldo
524 West 57th Street
New York, NY 10019
(212) 265-8520

Roberta Dougherty, Editorial Producer
Good Morning America
ABC-TV
1965 Broadway, 5th Floor
New York, NY 10023
(212) 496-4803

Don Navatto, Story Coordinator
Hard Copy
Fox Television Network
15 Columbus Circle
23rd Floor
New York, NY 10023
(212) 373-7600

Alex Williamson, Segment Producer
Joan Rivers Show
524 West 57th Street
New York, NY 10019
(212) 975-5522

Madeline Smithberg, Talent Coordinator
Late Night With David Letterman
NBC-TV
30 Rockefeller Plaza
New York, NY 10112
(212) 664-5908

Story Ideas
Nightline
ABC-TV
47 West 66th Street, 2nd Floor
New York, NY 10023
(212) 887-4995

Debbie DiMaio, Executive Producer
Oprah Winfrey Show
110 North Carpenter
Chicago, IL 60607
(312) 633-0808

Burt Dubrow, Executive Producer
Sally Jessy Raphael Show
510 West 57th Street
New York, NY 10019
(212) 582-1722

Robert Wheelock, Senior Producer
Today Show
NBC-TV
30 Rockefeller Plaza
New York, NY 10112
(212) 664-3127

Talent Coordinator
Tonight Show
NBC-TV
3000 West Alameda Avenue
Burbank, CA 91523
(818) 840-3676

INDEX